WHEN YOUR PARTNER HAS BIPOLAR DISORDER

William O. Selig, PsyD, MFA

when your partner has

bipolar disorder

helping you and your
partner build a balanced
and healthy relationship

**ROCKRIDGE
PRESS**

Interior and Cover Designer: Rachel Haeseker
Art Producer: Sue Bischofberger
Editor: Seth Schwartz and Samantha Holland
Production Editor: Andrew Yackira

Author photo courtesy of Sarah Lefton

ISBN: Print 978-1-64611-335-4 | eBook 978-1-64611-336-1
R1

To Sarah, Levi, Yali, and Ruth, with love

Contents

Introduction

I joined the field of psychology after more than a decade of working in the theater, directing, acting, and producing. The overlap between psychology and theater became immediately apparent: Both investigate the internal experiences that drive human behavior.

I was fascinated by bipolar disorder's long and turbulent history with artistic geniuses—from Vincent van Gogh to Jimi Hendrix to Ernest Hemingway. The condition's association with genius extends beyond artists, too: Winston Churchill, Ted Turner, Abbie Hoffman, and the list goes on. What was it about this illness that seemed to drive some of humankind's greatest accomplishments? Bipolar disorder's link to creativity was an interest shared by Dr. Terence Ketter, founder and chief of Stanford University's Bipolar Disorders Clinic, and I learned a great deal from both him and then–Associate Professor Dr. Jenifer Culver during my time there.

I quickly understood that working with people who have bipolar disorder—not studying them—was my passion, and there were many opportunities to do so throughout my graduate training. I cemented my clinical expertise with bipolar disorder during my postdoctoral residency and subsequent work at Kaiser Permanente Psychiatry & Behavioral Health in Oakland, California, which serves a large and diverse population. There, I had the opportunity to make an impact on a wider scale in collaboration with Andrea Glover, LCSW, who had developed a robust program of psychotherapy for bipolar disorder over many years at Kaiser. She enlisted me to help her revise the series of psychotherapy treatments offered for bipolar disorder there, and I undertook an exhaustive review of the existing scientific evidence about what works.

In my field, it doesn't take long to become known for clinical skill with bipolar disorder—it's a diagnosis that many therapists prefer not to work with due to its complexity. I soon found myself frequently working with people who struggle with the condition. Because bipolar disorder often impacts the person's partner and family, consulting with them also became one of my specialties.

Living with a partner who has bipolar disorder can feel daunting. It is a chronic mental health condition that is difficult to manage, but doing so *is* possible. This is particularly the case if the person with the condition is willing to face what the diagnosis means and seek out treatment while maintaining open communication with their loved ones.

This book is designed to help you and your partner build a healthy and balanced relationship by providing you with accurate, up-to-date information about bipolar disorder, as well as specific and effective tools, resources, and guidance. This book focuses on practical strategies for a broad spectrum of bipolar disorders, with information on the latest treatment plans, including medications and therapy. Technical language can be difficult to process, so I have avoided it as much as possible in this book. The References section (page 164) provides a deep dive into the scientific literature, if you are interested in further deepening your knowledge.

Reading about bipolar disorder and how to manage this condition may not be easy, but my hope is that this book will take you on a helpful and satisfying journey. You may be surprised or somewhat overwhelmed by the many different ways the illness can present itself or all the possible treatments, including medications and various therapeutic approaches. Keep in mind, however, that focusing too much or too long on analyzing your relationship is not healthy, and don't feel you need to read this book all at once. I offer specific suggestions for ways to de-stress and take time for yourself at the end of each chapter.

Many couples sustain happy and successful relationships despite the presence of a bipolar disorder diagnosis. Bipolar disorder or not, every couple has to work hard to build a strong and stable relationship. Facing a challenge together often brings partners closer rather than driving them apart. In the case of living with someone with bipolar disorder, there are many helpful approaches you can take to turn this obstacle into an opportunity to strengthen your relationship. This book will guide you through them.

How to Use This Book

This book contains concrete information about the nature of bipolar disorder, specific ways you can work with your partner to manage it, and the importance of taking care of yourself. This book is designed to support you, which begins with giving you the information you need to understand what your partner is experiencing and some of the issues they may be facing.

Each chapter focuses on a specific topic and presents short scenarios that illustrate various situations related to the topic. These examples are drawn from my clinical experience, though identifying information and other details have been changed to protect confidentiality. In addition to these stories, all chapters have a few common elements:

- **Talk About It:** Practical communication tips (types of language and tone to use) and scripts for what to say to your partner.

- **Write It Down:** Journaling/writing exercises that may be used individually or with your partner.

- **Take a Mindful Minute:** Mindfulness meditations, self-care suggestions, and calming exercises to help you deal with potential stressors related to the chapter topic.

I recommend that you read the chapters in order rather than skipping around. This book takes you on a linear journey in which you will gain a better understanding of the different types of bipolar disorder and their various symptoms, as well as how you can support your partner and encourage them to engage in treatment—and what to do if they refuse.

You will learn about the current treatments available for bipolar disorder and then move on to fostering teamwork and togetherness in your relationship, while seeking external and internal support for yourself. You will also learn concrete tools to figure out and communicate your boundaries, so you can protect your own needs and keep yourself and your loved ones safe.

If you have children or are considering having children, you will have a chance to plan for the complicated questions that arise around bipolar disorder. Finally, you will take stock of how your relationship is doing and assess your plan moving forward.

As you read, you will notice recurring themes that are important to keep in mind. First, there are many different kinds of bipolar disorder, and the person who has it is separate from the condition they are managing. Their identity is not synonymous with the condition. At the same time, while bipolar disorder can look very different from person to person, similar approaches are helpful in its management. These include critical roles for medication, therapy, a balanced lifestyle, avoidance of mood-altering substances, and stress reduction. Finally, successfully managing the illness together is all about self-knowledge, self-empowerment, and a commitment to self-care, both for your partner *and* for yourself.

Staying positive, loving, joyful, and accepting of your partner can have a crucial impact on your relationship. Remembering what attracted you to them in the first place can help you weather many storms and pave the way to a future of great happiness. I hope that reading this book will prove to be a positive turning point for you long into the future. Thank you for choosing to take this journey with me. Turn the page and let's begin.

Bipolar disorder is a serious medical condition. If bipolar disorder is a concern, your partner should be evaluated by a mental health professional, ideally a psychiatrist, who can provide a full assessment and treatment recommendations, including medication. Nothing in this book constitutes or should be interpreted as medical advice. Furthermore, because I am a psychologist and not a psychiatrist, specific information and recommendations about medication are beyond my scope of practice, even when providing individual treatment.

Chapter 1

Does My Partner Have Bipolar Disorder?

Perhaps your partner has been diagnosed with bipolar disorder and you're wondering what it all means. Or maybe you're still asking yourself if your partner has this condition. You may be wondering if the label even matters. What would that diagnosis mean for them? What would it mean for you? If you have children, what would it mean for your kids? If you've discussed these concerns with others, you have likely received more than one opinion. Perhaps you've even had the thought, *Maybe it's just me.*

By nature, bipolar disorder is hard to put a finger on. The question of whether or not your partner has bipolar disorder can be legitimately confusing, with many complicating factors, including reasons some individuals may or may not want the answer to be "yes." What's needed is factual information, reflection, and an open dialogue with your partner. In this chapter, I introduce some of the ways bipolar disorder can present itself by offering true-to-life examples. I also discuss how to make sense of your partner's behavior in light of the diagnosis, and I offer recommendations to guide you in talking to your partner about bipolar disorder.

Can You Relate?

One thing you probably know for sure is that you're worried. While bipolar disorder looks quite different from person to person, you may relate to one or more of the following stories, which are told from the perspective of a partner of someone with the condition. The following examples illustrate different types of bipolar disorder—bipolar I, bipolar II, cyclothymic disorder, and unspecified bipolar disorder, respectively—each of which are covered in greater detail in chapter 2.

Nadia

Nadia is in love with her work. It's something I've always known and loved about her, and I rarely resent it because she drops everything and is instantly by our side anytime the kids or I need her. She is the quintessential serial entrepreneur: creative, passionate, driven, and yes, impulsive. Her moods have always followed the ups and downs of her business ventures (or the other way around). Being her partner is stressful, but I'd be lying if I said I haven't also enjoyed the roller-coaster thrills.

The dark times are really dark, though. It was hard to watch after her last restaurant closed. I knew she was sad and angry, but I couldn't reach her, no matter how hard I tried. It was like living with a silent zombie in pajamas. Our 16-year-old had seen this before, and it's easy for her to just be a teenager and pretend not to notice, but I can't stand seeing her mother so unavailable to her own daughter. Nadia was either in bed, watching TV, or sitting blankly on the couch. Under no circumstances did she answer her phone or texts. I'd seen this kind of behavior before, but never for this long—it was a full year before she was back on her feet and acting like herself again.

I talked to Nadia's mom over the holidays and learned that this was not the first time she had stopped functioning for such a long period.

Her mom also told me that Nadia's grandmother had been diagnosed with "manic depression," and that Nadia had also been hospitalized when she was a teenager but never stuck with the medication. Nadia was furious when I asked her about this: "Oh, so now you think I'm crazy, too?" I didn't press.

A few months ago, as usual, she came back to life. I love having the old, elated Nadia back, with all her excitement and sociability, but she's been progressively more erratic and I'm worried something is seriously wrong. She talks a mile a minute about her new ventures, which are sounding increasingly grandiose. I'll find her pacing around and talking to herself, day and night. She stays later and later at work, and I know she's drinking there—I can smell the alcohol on her when she comes home. When I ask her why she's out late, she acts weird and paranoid, shushing me and saying that she's busy "protecting our interests." I tried to have a serious check-in with her last night, but she stormed off, shouting, "No one believes in me, not even you!"

Marcus

It's hard to be happy for Marcus when he's on top of the world like this, because I've also seen how low he can go. There have been days when he barely makes it up and out the door to work, and this can last for weeks on end. Somehow he does it, but at the end of the day, he comes straight home and crawls into bed. Right now, though, he is so full of life! He talks like a man who knows what he wants and he moves quickly, knocking out one project after another—all the stuff that piled up when he was feeling low and a few new projects, too. Plus, I can't complain about his sex drive; it's like when we were first dating all over again.

I try to stay present and enjoy it, because I know what's coming. When he gets hyped up like this, there's always a crash around the corner. His psychiatrist says that Marcus should reach out at this point, when he's all hyped up, but he gets mad when I suggest that. He says, "There's nothing wrong; this is actually me. Why do you all want to medicate me just because I'm feeling good?" It's confusing. He's up, he's down, sometimes he's kind of neither—which one is the "real" Marcus? I guess they all are.

Still, the way he is right now isn't normal; I know that. He's up at all hours working on home projects, then he gets up again at 4 a.m. to work more before heading off to the gym for a two-hour workout. He usually hates shopping and our budget is tight, but he comes home with something new every day—shoes, model trains, art supplies . . . Yesterday, it was a waffle iron—and he doesn't even like waffles. "But I know how much you love them," he explained as he made me one from scratch. Oh boy, I love that man. But he's not dependable, and he's no fun when he's down . . . Can I really stay with someone like this?

Louisa

Louisa won't take me seriously when I bring up bipolar disorder, but I think she should get checked out. "I'm just a moody person," she insists, or sometimes she'll say, "It's just PMS." But this isn't about her "getting in a mood" when something good or bad happens, and it doesn't track regularly with her period.

It's more like two different versions of Louisa, alternating back and forth from time to time. One week she's her "happy self," jazzed about life and super productive. A couple weeks later, she's low again—just negative and down in the dumps. Instead of working late, she'll lounge on the couch and watch TV with me. That part is actually kind of nice. I love her, moods and all, but it's hard not knowing who will be walking through the door around dinnertime.

It didn't used to be like this. She was actually very even-keeled in the early years of our relationship, but something changed in her mid-20s and it's been up and down ever since. We looked online at the diagnosis, and she doesn't really meet the criteria. It's like there's kind of a flavor of it, but she doesn't have the real thing. I just wish she would go see a psychiatrist and get it checked out.

Tim

I don't know what to think. My friend Aubrey said the other day that "Tim is totally bipolar," and that's the third time someone's said that to me. I know why they'd say it, I guess—every once in a while, he does get all hyped up and agitated, and it lasts for a week or two. But I've looked up bipolar disorder more than once, and it doesn't seem to fit. Aren't you supposed to have downswings, too, if you have it? Tim's never down or moody. He's generally just good-natured.

The only exception is when he gets revved up, and then he does get a bit touchy. Mostly he goes out with his buddies more often, and when he comes home, he's out in the garage all night working on one of his cars. I always figure he's cranky because he's not getting enough sleep. Then again, he doesn't seem tired—on the contrary, he hops around like a bunny and eats like a horse. Things get messier than usual, since he always decides to reorganize one thing or another.

Aubrey told me that her husband said Tim gets pretty reckless and wild when he's revved up. Apparently, Tim got into some kind of bragging match at the bar the other night, and he ended up in a drag race with the other guy. That's not like Tim. Except, according to Aubrey's husband, this wasn't the first time . . . I guess I've got to talk to him. Maybe he should see a doctor.

What Does It All Mean?

If you can relate to any of the stories in this chapter, one thing is for sure: It does *not* mean your partner has bipolar disorder. You've noticed some behaviors that suggest the diagnosis could be considered, and you're doing exactly the right thing—seeking information and guidance that's likely to be helpful. Recognize that you are coping effectively with a concern that's creating understandable anxiety for you.

Only an experienced mental health professional can provide an accurate diagnosis of bipolar disorder. Of all the well-known psychiatric disorders, bipolar disorder is one of the most complex, difficult to recognize, and difficult to treat. It is easily mistaken for other disorders, and vice versa. If the diagnosis is given in a crisis setting, such as an emergency room or inpatient psychiatric ward, always seek a second opinion in an outpatient setting, where a more comprehensive assessment can be conducted.

It is easy to leap to self-diagnosis or pronounce an "armchair diagnosis" of someone else because so many of the symptoms are similar to emotional fluctuations that everyone goes through. Most people have a limited understanding of the condition, associated with media portrayals of extreme or psychotic mania. They may know someone who has bipolar disorder and make the incorrect assumption that the condition looks the same from person to person. Often people call something bipolar disorder when what they're describing is a volatility that is part of one's personality—they may say something like, "They are *so* bipolar."

In the coming chapters, you'll gain a more in-depth and nuanced understanding of bipolar disorder, but you still can't—and shouldn't—try to be the expert on your partner's mental health. If you and your partner differ on whether they have the condition, talk to them and perhaps encourage them to see a mental health provider.

If your partner has bipolar disorder, the key to their future health will be full acceptance of the diagnosis and effective engagement in treatment. Facing bipolar disorder and responding effectively is not an easy task. Most people with the condition struggle to sustain engagement in treatment. Successful management is hard and often unrewarding in the short term. Your partner may be facing a change in lifestyle, which can be difficult to sustain.

If your partner refuses to seek treatment and stick with it, you will have to learn to cope with the roller coaster of their bipolar disorder symptoms and their consequences. You may have to protect yourself from dangerous behavior. You may even have to cut ties with your partner for the sake of your safety and emotional health and that of others who live with you, and that's okay. However you react and respond is understandable—you need to look after yourself and your children (if you have them), first and foremost.

You probably wish all this uncertainty and fear would go away. Still, if your partner does have bipolar disorder, finding that out sooner rather than later will be enormously helpful. It could mean several different things—many of them good, not bad—for them, for you, and for the future. Remember to give yourself credit for the way that you're paying attention, with care and concern, noticing what matters to you.

While bipolar disorder is a worthy adversary, the simple fact that it presents a challenge in your relationship is not a reason to give up. Believe it or not, your relationship may become stronger for it, because uniting against a common enemy tends to bring people closer. You and your partner can join in facing a challenge that doesn't have to overwhelm your relationship. You can see it for what it is: an obstacle that is also an opportunity.

Write It Down

You may want to keep a new journal that's dedicated to supporting your partner with bipolar disorder and to respond to the exercises in this book. It may not be comfortable for either of you that you are journaling about your partner's bipolar disorder, and this could be upsetting for them—especially if it comes as a surprise. Be thoughtful about whether and how to share this journal with them. You have the right to keep it private, but ideally, it will not be a secret forever, and you and your partner will figure out how best to share ▶

your experience of their bipolar disorder. This book helps you build a framework of communication in which the journal can be discussed.

With that said, the journal can help you and/or your partner track what's happening with regard to their bipolar disorder as it progresses over time. The changes your partner goes through may be slow and subtle, so this is the best way to help you pay attention and remember what has occurred.

Because mood episodes—the highs or lows of bipolar disorder—can attack perception and insight (and even if they didn't), your partner will experience things differently than you do. Don't try to prove anything to them using the journal. Write observations that are objective, specific, and concrete. Pay attention to your partner's extremes in behavior, substance use, sleep patterns, and indicators of a shift in mood. Watch for changes that last several days in a row. Note environmental factors as well, such as events and other stressors.

You can also use this journal (or a separate one) to write about your subjective feelings, including your softer and more difficult feelings, like fear, hurt, or sadness. Painful as they are, these feelings are important. More than anything, sharing how your partner's bipolar disorder makes you feel will be the key to engaging with them in a productive way that helps your relationship take hold of the condition rather than the other way around.

What Should I Do Next?

Facing bipolar disorder with your partner is an ongoing journey. Informing yourself first, as you're doing right now, is a good start. You may want to do more research, talk to others who are knowledgeable, or consider going to a support group (more on this in chapter 6 and in the Resources section). It may help to talk with others who know your partner well—perhaps their family or close friends. As you collect information, don't wait too long to share your concerns with your partner. They may be upset if they think you've been talking about them behind their back or have been quietly using the diagnosis to explain their behavior to yourself.

It's not hard to weaponize this diagnosis ("Go take your meds" or "This is just you being bipolar!"), and if others have targeted or dismissed your partner for having the condition, they will have their defenses at the ready. They will be especially triggered if they feel you've joined forces with someone who has done this in the past. To work with your partner as a team, it's vital they understand that you are on their side. Coming directly to them with your concerns, and owning them as *your* concerns, will encourage them to collaborate with you and see you as their friend, not their enemy.

This book focuses on the needs of a person whose partner has bipolar disorder. First things first, you need information to help you understand what your partner is facing if they struggle with this condition. Chapter 2 provides this, detailing what bipolar disorder looks like, its symptoms, how it works, and the four most common subtypes in this class of psychiatric disorders.

Chapter 3 addresses how to support your partner and especially how to encourage them to engage in treatment. It addresses what to do if your partner refuses to get professional help. It also covers what to do if your partner is self-harming or suicidal.

Chapter 4 breaks down the various treatments available for bipolar disorder. There are many ways to treat it, with different approaches employed by various providers. Knowing the range of treatments available will help you support your loved one in making informed decisions.

Chapter 5 will help you build a foundation for ongoing collaborative management of bipolar disorder with your partner. You'll learn how to support your partner's action plan, so you can anticipate challenges and be prepared to intervene as needed. This chapter will also help you understand and empathize with your partner's struggle to manage their bipolar disorder.

Chapter 6 focuses on emotional challenges that may arise for you as a result of your partner's illness. There are suggestions of ways to seek external support and bolster the ways you support yourself. A crucial part of this involves observing your own limits, and chapter 7 addresses this. You'll find concrete tools to set boundaries that work for you. This chapter also addresses what to do if your partner's behavior becomes out of control.

Chapter 8 addresses the complicated questions that arise around children and bipolar disorder. You'll receive guidance on how to talk to children about the condition. The chapter also goes over questions you may have about having children with a partner who has bipolar disorder.

Chapter 9 provides a framework to take stock of your relationship: what's working and what's not, what could change and what probably won't. This chapter will help you work through the painful and understandable thoughts you may have if and when you consider ending your relationship.

In Real Life

After five minutes of researching on the internet, Aika was convinced that June had bipolar disorder. Afraid to say anything, she held her tongue and spent a couple days collecting more information. This diagnosis was complicated! Having thought out her approach, she sat down calmly with June to talk about it. She was relieved and impressed with the response! June was actually interested in the information Aika had gathered and decided to make an appointment to see a doctor.

Talk About It

If you've never talked about bipolar disorder with your partner before, you'll need to gauge how receptive they are. Here are some tips on how to dip your toe in the water:

Find a good time to bring it up. Don't choose a time when tensions are high. Let them know you want to have a conversation that may be uncomfortable and ask if or when they'd be available for that.

Lead with softer feelings. Express your love and perhaps your fear that bringing up this subject could hurt their feelings or make them angry.

Emphasize that you bring this up from a place of caring and with the best intentions. Ask them to give you the benefit of the doubt and to try to listen openly and without becoming defensive.

Approach with humility. Use phrases like "I'm no expert . . . ," "I really don't know . . . ," and "I'm wondering if . . . ."

Adopt a stance of curiosity and openness. Ask "What do you think?" and "How does it feel to hear me say this?" Give them the space they need to respond. Listen and don't argue. No matter what, validate their feelings by acknowledging them and not trying to change them. If they react angrily or in a way you weren't expecting, you can say, "Okay, I understand you don't want to talk about this," or "I get that you don't appreciate me bringing this up."

Be patient. You won't reach agreement on everything. All you're doing is opening up a conversation. Don't insist on anything beyond keeping the line of communication open. "Let me sit with what you've said. I may ask if we can talk about it another time. Would that be okay?"

Take a Mindful Minute

Take a moment to give yourself credit for doing this hard work. Instead of denying, blaming, or avoiding, you are facing your fears and gathering more information. This will reduce your anxiety and give you the tools to be a more effective and supportive partner. Still, that doesn't mean this isn't stressful work. It's your partner's great fortune to have someone in their life (that's you I'm talking about!) working hard to understand them. Remind yourself that, as hard a time as they may be having, this is hard on you, too.

To support other people, you have to "put your own oxygen mask on first." This means making space and time—actual minutes, hours, and days—for self-compassion and self-care. As a way of encouraging you to make more space for this in your life, the end of every chapter will prompt you to take a moment for yourself. You can use these strategies anytime you need a break.

For now, find a quiet place to sit or lie down where you won't be disturbed. Take a deep breath, imagining that your belly is a balloon. As you suck air in through your nose, the balloon in your belly fills all the way up, and as you push the air out through your mouth, the balloon deflates. This is called "belly breathing," and it brings in much more oxygen and relaxation than the breathing we often do using our chest muscles within a tense abdomen.

Take five deep and complete "belly breaths."

Chapter 2

Understanding Bipolar Disorder

The hallmark of bipolar disorder is variation. No two people have exactly the same symptoms or experience the same twists and turns in life. In essence, though, every version of the condition involves variation along three key lines: mood, energy, and activity.

After reading this chapter, you will come to better understand the nature of bipolar disorder. I will explain it using the metaphor of a playground seesaw and the concept of a continuum or spectrum. You will learn about the various mood states, including mania and depression. Finally, you will discover the various types of bipolar disorder, and I will go over the details of the most commonly given diagnoses. This chapter includes a lot of information that can be difficult to sort out, but bipolar disorder is complicated. Better understanding its complexity will help you understand your partner's diagnosis and ultimately strengthen your relationship.

What Does Bipolar Disorder Look Like?

Bipolar disorder involves changes in brain chemistry that cycle unpredictably over time. The cycles cause shifts among three basic mood states: depressed, hypomanic/manic, and euthymic. A *euthymic mood* is a state of wellness; it still includes emotional ups and downs, but they are within the individual's own "normal" range. When bipolar disorder takes a person out of their euthymic range into one of the other mood states, their behavior becomes noticeably different and their perceptions, insight, and judgment may become altered or impaired. All of this affects their ability to function, sometimes for the better but more frequently for the worse.

Bipolar disorder is a chronic, lifetime condition, meaning that once it emerges, it cannot be cured. It can emerge at any time of life, but it is most commonly recognized and diagnosed in people ages 15 to 35; the average age of onset is 25. There is a clear genetic component: First-degree relatives of a person with bipolar disorder are 10 times more likely to develop the condition than the general population. At the same time, it can also emerge when it has never been seen before in a family.

In casual conversation, we sometimes use the word *mood* to describe an emotional state that might last a few hours. This kind of "good mood" or "bad mood" often follows from a particular event. The mood shifts of bipolar disorder, on the other hand, come in extended episodes. They are not like the ups and downs we all experience. Rather, a mood episode involves an extended period of time when the unusual state persists, regardless of positive or negative events.

Depending on the person and the episode, mood shifts in bipolar disorder can have different qualities. On the low side, a person may experience a "depressed" mood, which could feel to them like sadness, hopelessness, or emptiness. On the other hand, they may simply feel "flat," taking little interest or pleasure in much of anything. They could feel some combination of all of these things. They may appear tearful, but they may also appear agitated, irritable, slowed down, or unresponsive.

When a person with bipolar disorder is "up," they will feel increased energy and/or engage in increased activity. They may feel elated, expansive, or "on a high." They might also feel irritable. They may have increased self-esteem or creativity and may appear abnormally excited or impassioned.

With bipolar disorder, there is variability at every level. One person's symptoms may look nothing like another's. Even the typical cluster of symptoms that one person experiences can change over time. The illness takes an unpredictable course throughout the person's life, with the frequency and intensity of episodes often changing. One person might have one or two episodes in their entire life, while another experiences multiple episodes in a year. People respond differently to medications and therapy, and even if a particular intervention works well, it can become ineffective later on. This is one of many reasons it is important to have an ongoing relationship with a psychiatrist, and it is helpful to work consistently with a therapist as well.

To simplify things, let's say that bipolar disorder operates a bit like a seesaw. A seesaw goes up and down within a limited range—no matter how hard you push, one side can only go so high and the other side can only go so low, and the seesaw's basic functioning remains intact. When bipolar disorder first emerges, the seesaw careens up or down beyond its usual range, breaking through the limits that had always held it in balance. Even after the seesaw returns to its usual range, the bolts in the pivot point have permanently loosened. This looseness is the condition we call bipolar disorder, the vulnerability to again swing deeper or shoot higher than usual, sometimes with the barest of nudges.

One of the most frustrating aspects of the illness is this: Each episode tends to further loosen the bolts of the seesaw, increasing the risk of a future episode, as well as its likely severity. Each episode also increases the illness's resistance to treatment and makes recovery more difficult by creating problems that compound over time: increased debt, burnt bridges, and lost opportunities. Without treatment and active management, the seesaw will find stability harder and harder to achieve.

The good news is that active monitoring and well-informed management can be enormously powerful and effective. If your partner learns to watch out for swings and intervene early, they can spend more time within their "normal" range and maybe even avoid episodes altogether. Because each person's bipolar disorder is so different, maintaining stability and early intervention are all about self-knowledge and self-empowerment. This is why research has shown again and again that, in combination with medication, learning about bipolar disorder is one of the most effective treatments for it. There's even a fancy word for this kind of treatment: *psychoeducation.* Guess who's engaging in it right now, the very thing that's proven to help? You are.

In Real Life

Nancy has raised the question of bipolar disorder with Hector before. It pains her to watch his long periods of sadness and low motivation. They are in such high contrast with the sudden, weeklong bursts of energy he displays from time to time. Hector has argued Nancy out of this speculation in the past. His mother had bipolar disorder, and he says, "She was crazy—I'm nothing like her." Having done more research, though, Nancy now again wonders if Hector has the condition—maybe his version is just different?

The Bipolar Spectrum

To truly understand bipolar disorder, it's useful to know why mental health providers increasingly refer to the "bipolar spectrum" when talking about the illness. The reason lies in the distinction between continua and categories, which are two different ways to describe difference. For example, let's look at temperature. When ordering at a sandwich shop, you might think in categories: *Do I want a hot or a cold sandwich?*

But if a child has a fever, you will measure their temperature—not because you want to know whether they fit in the 101.7°F or the 103.2°F category, but rather to get a sense of where they are on a continuum of possible temperatures (roughly 97°F to 105°F). You will most likely take the measurement more than once, because you want to know whether their temperature is going up or going down. You will also consider a variety of other symptoms, such as fatigue or headaches, each of which exists on a continuum of severity. As the illness emerges, worsens, and goes away, you will describe it over time by using these symptom continua: "Their fever is down from yesterday, and they're less congested, but their cough is worse." This is where the concept of a spectrum comes into play: As it develops, your child's illness moves in its own particular way through a broad spectrum of "the flu."

The following figure illustrates the difference between a categorical view and a view that looks at things as a continuum/spectrum.

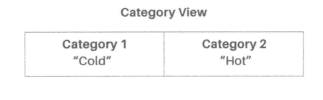

Category View

Category 1 "Cold"	Category 2 "Hot"

vs.

Continuum/Spectrum View

Lower Temperature "Colder"	Average Temperature	Higher Temperature "Hotter"

Figure 1. Two different perspectives: categories versus continua/spectrums

Categorical descriptions are more useful when details are less important (such as "salty" or "sweet"). Categories also make distinctions that are clear and simple (lights "on" or "off"). A continuum works best in describing a level of intensity or something that changes gradually along a gradient, like a light on a dimmer. A spectrum might describe whether that light is emitted by a "soft white," "daylight," or "bright light" bulb.

Diagnoses are categories by definition, but thinking of bipolar disorder only as a category is too limiting. Just as experiencing a "real summer day" represents an intersection of continua (temperature, humidity, precipitation, wind, and more), the progression over time of bipolar disorder involves multiple symptom continua. Furthermore, these symptoms combine to form a spectrum that is broad and complex. A "real summer day" in Minnesota is completely different from one in Texas, and each person's bipolar disorder has its own particular climate. This is why mental health providers increasingly describe people as having a "bipolar spectrum disorder" or being on the "bipolar spectrum" rather than using the traditional categorical diagnoses.

Still, using categories as a means of description can be useful. Diagnoses help providers communicate quickly and easily, know what medications are appropriate, and reference resources that guide effective treatment. In addition, while many people struggle to accept a diagnosis of bipolar disorder, others find the category helpful. It recognizes and validates why they have struggled, helps them realize that they are not alone, and provides hope that the condition is known and treatable.

The official criteria for a diagnosis of bipolar disorder can be found in the American Psychiatric Association's *Diagnostic and Statistical Manual of Mental Disorders*, 5th Edition (DSM-5). The descriptions in the following section use language from the DSM-5.

What Is Mania?

Mania is an extreme state of mood elevation. Most media depictions of bipolar disorder are sensational, dramatizing a person in the most severe version of this state, which includes psychosis, a state of mind disconnected from reality. Mania is not always so severe. Indeed, we can best understand it by first understanding its milder form, *hypomania*.

Hypomania represents a noticeable change from usual behavior and includes a shift in mood (more elevated, expansive, or irritable), and an increase in either energy or activity. It also includes some of the following symptoms:

- Sleeping less, but still feeling energized

- Increased self-esteem

- More talkative than usual

- Racing thoughts or *flight of ideas* (moving quickly from one to another unrelated thought)

- Distractable

- Physically restless

- Increased high-risk/pleasurable activities (such as excessive spending or sexual indiscretions)

Turning now from hypomania to mania, you will see the relevance of the spectrum model: The symptoms of mania and hypomania are identical. The only difference is that the symptoms of mania are exaggerated to the point that they cause "marked impairment," as the DSM-5 states. Once people enter full-blown mania, they may be hospitalized or become psychotic. Because hypomania and mania develop along a spectrum, I prefer to refer to both as simply "mood elevation." I specify mania only when an episode has clearly crossed that line.

Hypomania doesn't impair functioning; it frequently enhances it. When hypomanic, people may be more creative, more productive, more self-confident, and more social. They may start more projects than they can ultimately sustain. As long as they're not experiencing too much irritability or physical agitation, though, they tend to feel fantastic.

Understandably, people with bipolar disorder don't want to give this up, and this is frequently the biggest obstacle to engaging in treatment. Given the painful depressions they suffer, people with bipolar disorder often feel that hypomania is the one silver lining of their condition. Sometimes they intentionally induce it through sleep deprivation or substance abuse, for instance, hoping they can sustain the state.

While we can't blame folks for chasing hypomania, they are entering dangerous territory for three reasons:

- They are sabotaging successful treatment of their illness.

- They are increasing their risk of depression, which tends to follow mood elevation.

- They may continue up the spectrum to full-blown mania, even if this has never happened to them before.

Unlike hypomania, full-blown manic episodes impair functioning and can lead to disastrous outcomes. Manic episodes often don't feel good and are frequently accompanied by anxiety or irritability. As the intensity rises, symptoms that were pleasurable become frightening and overwhelming. The elevated state can rev up quickly: Happy becomes euphoric, which becomes grandiose, which then suddenly becomes psychotic.

The state of psychosis also emerges on a continuum of varying intensity. Full-blown psychosis is described as *florid*. It typically includes beliefs (delusions) and sensory perceptions (hallucinations) that are not based in reality. Florid psychosis is frequently accompanied by agitation or incoherent speech and behavior.

Some people report transcendent, ecstatic states of feeling "connected" or even godlike during mania, but psychosis is typically frightening for all involved because the psychotic individual is living in an "alternate reality." If your partner becomes psychotic, trying to talk them out of irrational beliefs and perceptions will be counterproductive. Instead, focus on their basic needs (hydration, food, and rest) and tend to their emotions by soothing them and helping them feel safe while seeking immediate evaluation by a health professional.

What Is Depression?

Like mania, depression in bipolar disorder is frequently misunderstood. People may describe themselves as feeling "depressed," but that does not mean they are experiencing a major depressive episode (MDE). They are usually describing a set of emotions like feeling sad, dejected, discouraged, or "blue," often in the wake of an identifiable trigger. Emotions like these may be a part of an MDE, but far more is needed to meet the MDE criteria.

It may surprise you to learn that clinical depression doesn't always involve feeling sad. An MDE always includes a shift in mood, but this can show up as irritability or *anhedonia*, which is a general loss of interest or pleasure. People with anhedonia report feeling "flat" and unmotivated, even by activities they usually love.

The main difference, though, between MDEs and the way many people sometimes feel "depressed" is that MDEs occur over an extended period of time. We all get down about life sometimes, exhibiting "symptoms" like those of an MDE.

However, we tend to recover from this feeling within hours or days, especially if something happens to raise our spirits. This is not the case with an MDE.

An MDE is a biochemical state in which there is a general damper on everything. It can last most of the day, nearly every day, for at least two weeks and sometimes for years. Even a raise at work, for instance, might be hard to enjoy. Depressive thoughts might twist this quickly into a reason to feel guilty or worthless; instead of going out to celebrate, a person in the throes of an MDE might just go home and crawl into bed.

To meet criteria for an MDE, a person must exhibit either low mood or anhedonia. They may also experience:

- Loss of energy

- An increase *or* decrease in appetite or weight

- Difficulty sleeping *or* hypersomnia (sleeping longer, taking naps)

- Physical restlessness

- Slowed movement or speech, slumped posture, staring into space

- Difficulty concentrating or making decisions

- Self-critical thoughts

- Suicidal thoughts

MDEs have no distinction comparable to mood elevation's hypomania versus mania. Clinicians describe MDEs as mild, moderate, or severe; regardless of severity, there are no upsides to depression. MDEs tend to emerge more slowly than mood elevations, allowing them to sneak up on a person. That said, observing your partner over time will make it easier to see an MDE coming, creating an opportunity to intervene before it gets worse. The most common observable warning signs include:

- Decreased energy
- Lack of motivation
- Irritability
- Change in sleep patterns

In Real Life

Camila can always tell when Jaime begins to feel low: Dishes begin to pile up in the sink. He doesn't seem sad, just unexcited and "checked out." He starts pulling out of social dates at the last minute. It's been worse before, with weeks on end when he barely gets out of bed, but things seem to be worsening and he's saying things like "There's no point" and "I wish I was dead." Camila overcomes her hesitation and asks Jaime to check in with his psychiatrist.

Write It Down

Since every version of bipolar disorder is different, it's important to learn what your partner's particular version looks like. In your journal, write about the behaviors and symptoms you observe when your partner's mood is depressed and when their mood is elevated. In the following section, you'll be prompted to talk with your partner about their experience of these mood states. You can share your specific, concrete, and factual observations, but keep in mind that many of these symptoms are internal and subjective. After you talk with your partner about their experience, make some notes in your journal about what you have learned.

Talk About It

Helping your partner manage their bipolar disorder means improving your ability to join them in monitoring their changing mood symptoms. In this chapter, you are becoming familiar with some of the jargon doctors use. Over time, though, you and your partner will develop your own shared language to check in about their mood.

Explain that you've learned that people with bipolar disorder have widely varying experiences and you want to understand your partner's own specific experience. Ask your partner the following questions:

- "How do you know when you're having a depressive episode or experiencing mood elevation?"

- "Are there early warning signs you notice when an episode is coming on?"

- "When I see you doing [insert action here], it makes me wonder if that means an episode is coming on. What do you think?"

As always, humility and open curiosity are key. Focus on asking questions and listening. Stick with the words your partner uses, so they don't feel like you're defining their experience for them. When you approach your partner in this positive, unassuming way, they will feel supported by your interest and respect, and you will learn more about how to help your partner monitor their illness.

The Bipolar Disorder Diagnosis

Although bipolar disorder can be diagnosed by any licensed mental health professional, the eventual involvement of a psychiatrist is essential. The condition is driven by biochemical mechanisms in the brain, and therefore a medical doctor (in this case, a psychiatrist) is required to direct assessment and treatment. The medications that exist for treating bipolar disorder are far from perfect, but they remain the recommended first-line treatment. Psychotherapy can also play an important role in treating bipolar disorder, providing support in a variety of ways.

The mood charts in this section will help you envision the categorical diagnoses of bipolar disorder. Each graph illustrates a sample pattern of changing mood states over the course of five years, but remember, this is just one example. Your partner's illness will take its own course. Time is represented on the bottom (x-axis), while the mood states are represented on the left (y-axis).

Bipolar I

The defining feature of bipolar I disorder is the presence of at least one full-blown manic episode. If your partner has bipolar I, they will very likely also experience major depressive episodes (MDEs) as well as periods of hypomania. Here is one example of what a bipolar I disorder might look like over time:

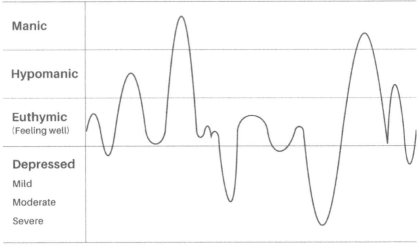

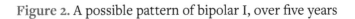

Figure 2. A possible pattern of bipolar I, over five years

The previous mood chart might reflect the first five years of bipolar disorder for someone like Nadia (page 2). Perhaps her first hypomanic episode went unrecognized, but the second mood elevation landed her in the hospital. Her first MDE followed the mania, and her second mania was a rebound from a dark depression.

The next mood chart is a very different progression of bipolar I. This person would experience chronic and persistent low mood (or *dysthymia*) interrupted by an MDE, which then rebounds into full-blown mania before settling back into the usual dysthymia. Future mood episodes may follow.

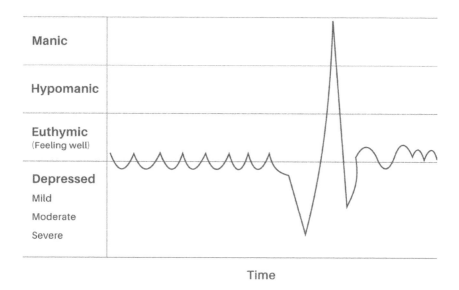

Figure 3. A very different pattern of bipolar I, over five years

Bipolar II

For a diagnosis of bipolar II disorder, a person must have at least one MDE and one hypomanic episode, with no history of full-blown mania. People with bipolar II may still develop a manic episode, in which case their diagnosis will change to bipolar I. Over five years, Marcus's bipolar II disorder (page 3) might look something like this:

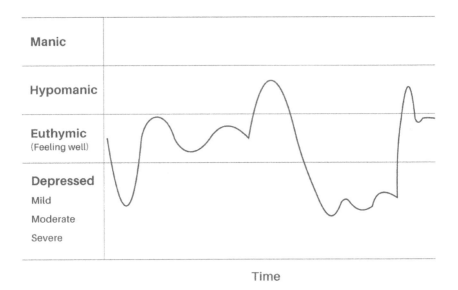

Figure 4. Possible pattern of bipolar II, over five years

Cyclothymic Disorder

Cyclothymic disorder is a milder form of bipolar disorder. To meet this diagnosis, multiple episodes over two years must show symptoms of depression or mood elevation, without ever meeting full criteria for a major depressive or hypomanic episode. Louisa's cyclothymia (page 4) might look something like this:

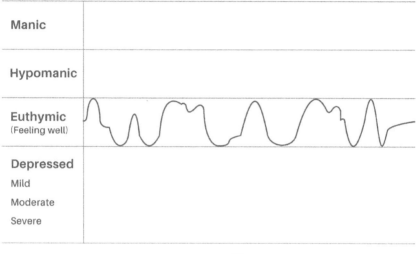

Figure 5. Possible pattern of cyclothymic disorder, over five years

Unspecified Bipolar Disorder

The diagnosis of unspecified bipolar and related disorder describes bipolar spectrum disorders where the distressing symptoms don't meet full criteria for any of the other diagnoses. Tim's example (page 5) might qualify—he's had multiple hypomanic episodes but no MDEs, so he can't be diagnosed with bipolar II. The unspecified bipolar disorder diagnosis may also be given when clinicians don't have enough information to be more specific (such as in an emergency room).

Ruling Out Other Diagnoses

Other psychiatric illnesses may sometimes look similar to bipolar disorder's mania or depression. Chief among these is major depressive disorder (MDD, or unipolar depression). People with MDD have recurring major depressive episodes but no episodes of mood elevation. A number of other serious psychiatric conditions can also include the psychotic features that may accompany both mania and severe depression (delusions, hallucinations, disorganized speech, disorganized or catatonic behavior). These include schizophrenia, substance-induced psychotic disorder, and schizoaffective disorder, which may also include high and low fluctuations in mood. The need to rule out these other conditions is among the many reasons bipolar disorder should be thoroughly evaluated by a psychiatrist.

Take a Mindful Minute

This chapter has covered the most challenging aspects of bipolar disorder. Learning about this condition can feel overwhelming or stressful, especially when you're worried (or know) that your partner has it. Give yourself the time you need to absorb the information. Know that in the chapters to come, you will find guidance and many tools to help you cope and manage this challenge.

If you're experiencing anxiety or worry about the future, here is one way to try to let go. Remind yourself that your thoughts are just that: thoughts. You don't know what will happen nor is it happening yet. The only thing that is happening right now is . . . right now. To quickly ground yourself in the moment, look around the space you are in and name out loud or to yourself:

- **Five** things you can see

- **Four** things you can hear

- **Three** things you can touch

- **Two** things you can smell

- **One** thing you can taste

You can do this anytime your thoughts are taking you out of the present moment. It takes only a minute, but its calming effects can be long-lasting.

Chapter 3

Supporting Your Partner

This chapter is about supporting your partner, but it's also about supporting you, too. The very fact that you want to be supportive is in and of itself supportive. Whether or not your partner expresses appreciation for your efforts (and especially if they don't), give yourself the compassion and love you deserve for your efforts. If your partner pushes back at times or even gets angry at you for trying to support them, this is unfortunate but not unusual. In this chapter, we'll talk about how to handle these kinds of reactions, how to understand what kind of support your partner needs, and how to offer it effectively.

Encouraging Your Partner to Seek Help

One of the best ways for you to help your partner is to encourage them to begin, and stay engaged in, treatment. Successful management of bipolar disorder involves taking medication, seeing a psychiatrist, and most likely working with a therapist. Getting into treatment and staying engaged isn't easy. If your partner doesn't struggle with this, that's very good news. If they do, they've doubtless resisted pressure about it from others and they may not want to experience this again from you. This puts you in a tough position if you think they need help. There are a number of specific strategies, however, that will help you be effective:

Emphasize your feelings. Sharing that "I'm feeling scared" can be useful. Even if they disagree that seeing a professional could be helpful, you can frame it as something you're asking them to do so you can rest easy. Convey that you are talking to them about this because you care. Help them understand that you know they're trying hard and doing their best, that you love and accept them for who they are, and that you don't blame them for their struggles.

Avoid using clinical language or suggesting a diagnosis. No one enjoys being diagnosed with a mental illness, even by an objective professional. Coming from you, even if you don't mean it this way, a diagnosis could imply that you bear no responsibility for problems you and your partner are having. In the context of a conflict, no one wants to hear, "You're sick." Remember, from your partner's perspective, you're telling them there's something about their behavior that you think they need help changing—this can be tough to hear.

If your partner brings up the diagnosis, don't agree too quickly. They may feel ambivalent and want to discuss it with you in an open way. If they tell you they've been diagnosed with bipolar disorder, a helpful first question would be, "Do you agree with the diagnosis?" I always keep in mind—and remind my patients as well—that they are the experts on themselves. They must come to their own conclusions about what they're going through.

Ask if and how they would like to receive information or hear your thoughts before sharing them. If you have resources, information, observations, or opinions to share, first ask if your partner would like to hear them. Respect their wishes. If you want them to seek professional help, own that as your own desire and practice humility: What they need or should do is a matter of opinion, and treatment will not be helpful unless they actively want it. Remember, your aim is to get them to seek help, not convince them that they have bipolar disorder.

If they don't want to see a psychiatrist, start with a therapist. Your partner may be scared or dead set against medication. Accept this and ask them to talk with a therapist instead. Using the word *counselor* may be even less threatening. You don't need to convince your partner to start medication (and you might be wrong about them needing it). Focus on getting them engaged somehow with a mental health provider they trust who can give them professional advice.

Double down on basic communication skills. Be gentle and calm in your approach. Stick with specific, objective, and concrete observations. Stay away from words like *always* and *never*, and use "I" statements ("When you . . . I feel . . ."). The less you talk, the better: Listen to their responses, ask questions, and listen more. The more you listen, the more weight your words will have. Respond to what they say with "It sounds like . . ." and repeat back to them what you think they said. Accept any corrections they offer. Validate their feelings—for example, say, "I understand why you would feel that way," or "I would feel the same way." You can have your opinion and still say, "I understand why you're upset. I'm sorry I hurt your feelings."

Sometimes it's necessary to back off. If your partner is resistant to seeking help or starts to get agitated, let them know that you respect their decision and back off. It's perfectly fine to take a break—you want them to associate having this kind of conversation with loving and supportive feelings, not negative ones. It will be unproductive if they feel you are trying to force them to do something or if they feel you won't accept their choice. However, if the issue is unresolved, let them know you'd like to return to the topic at a later time.

Practice patience. It may take more than one conversation. Depending on where your partner is in their process of acceptance, their agreement to at least think about getting help may be a big win, and they may not even agree to that. Try to accept and empathize—out loud—with their resistance or ambivalence, remaining open and nonjudgmental about their opinion.

In Real Life

Suzanne has tried to get Rick to see a counselor before, but he doesn't believe in "airing his dirty laundry." Now his insomnia is back, and during the day he does nothing but pad in his slippers from the couch to the kitchen and back. He talks about how overwhelmed he is by work, but he doesn't do anything to catch up. Suzanne can't take it anymore—she knows he needs help!

What If My Partner Won't Seek Help?

If you're frustrated by your partner's resistance to seek treatment, you are not alone. Even if they have been in treatment or taken medication before, they may drop out, forget to take their medication, or be opposed to starting again. They may have been told they will need to take medication for the rest of their lives, which can be hard for anyone to accept. Unfortunately, resistance to treatment recommendations is extremely common for people struggling with bipolar disorder—it goes with the territory.

During, or directly following, a mood episode, your partner will likely be more motivated for treatment, but once they've been stable for a while, they may decide they don't need it anymore. The longer they stay stable after stopping their medication (which could be years), the more convinced they will be that they didn't need it after all. All too often, though, they eventually realize the doctors were right once it's too late to prevent another episode.

In trying to understand this, people often focus on the challenges involved in treatment—side effects, hassle and cost of appointments, lifestyle restrictions, etc. These are significant deterrents, particularly the cost-benefit dilemma that comes with medication. Recommended lifestyle changes (e.g., regularity of sleep, diet, schedule, exercise, abstinence from drugs and alcohol, etc.) can also feel overwhelming. As one of my patients asked when I explained these recommendations to them, "What am I supposed to do, live like a monk?"

If your partner resists treatment, it may also be due to negative experiences they've had in the past with mental health providers. This is especially likely if your partner has been hospitalized, which can be an uncomfortably impersonal and traumatic experience. They may be alienated from the very health-care system that exists to help them. If your partner feels this way, try to remind them that every provider is different. If they're seeing someone for the first time, it can make all the difference if they tell them what kind of treatment has or hasn't worked for them in the past.

Beyond the challenges of treatment, however, many people who have been diagnosed with bipolar disorder don't believe it or can't recognize it. Even if they believe the diagnosis is accurate, they may think they don't need medication or any other kind of help. They may find a variety of reasons not to accept or follow the treatment recommendations they've received from mental health providers.

Imagine this: One day, out of the blue, you're in a doctor's office being informed that you have a chronic, incurable, life-threatening, heavily stigmatized illness that's been hijacking your life without your knowledge. On top of that, you're told you have to take medication for the rest of your life. You try the pills, but they affect your mood, energy, and perceptions in ways you're not at all sure you like, or they come with side effects you never imagined would be part of your daily experience. "Normalcy" has been yanked from you forever and without warning; the shock of this extraordinary loss would be immense. As the shock wore off, your feelings about this loss would begin to manifest through the grief process.

Psychiatrist Elisabeth Kübler-Ross laid out the five "stages of grief" in her book *On Death and Dying.* Subsequent research has shown her model to be an inaccurate general- ization of grief, but it's interesting in our context because her ideas developed through studying patients who received a diagnosis of terminal cancer. She was describing how they felt, not about a loved one that they lost, but about the loss of the future they had imagined for themselves. The stages she named were denial, anger, bargaining (trying to find a way out of the loss), depression, and acceptance. While these stages don't occur in a linear fashion, you may recog- nize some or all of these in your loved one's response to their diagnosis. So, what exactly are they grieving?

A diagnosis of bipolar disorder strikes at the core of a person's identity. Our moods and emotions are central to our sense of self and our ideas about life and reality. Your part- ner's depressions and episodes of mood elevation are part of who they are, but they're being told that this part of them is sick. It's particularly hard to accept this with regard to hypomania; these times are when your partner probably feels their best, so it's hard for them to see them as something wrong that must be "treated" out of existence.

If your partner has bipolar disorder, they face the unan- swerable question: "Which me is me?" With so much stigma and misunderstanding surrounding bipolar disorder, they've been classified and lumped into an unfavorable category, with all sorts of negative implications for how society will view and treat them. This denies their individual humanity and has the potential to reduce their entire being to a sickness—one in which something is deeply wrong with who they are.

When you consider all of this, you can get a sense of what your partner is grieving. They are grieving the loss of the "normal" life they once thought lay ahead of them. They are grieving who they thought they were, as well as their hopes and dreams. On some level, they know they desperately need help, but it seems accepting that means embracing the unacceptable. The back and forth of engaging and disengaging from treatment is an expression of this grief and ambivalence that Kübler-Ross described as "bargaining."

These thoughts are harrowing, I know. But there is good news: The catastrophic future in your partner's mind is a fear, not a reality. They don't need to grieve what they haven't yet lost. They are still the same person they have always been. Many people with bipolar disorder lead ordinary, even extraordinary lives. In fact, bipolar disorder is more common among famous achievers than it is among the general population, including the likes of singer Mariah Carey, astronaut Buzz Aldrin, and so many more. The incredible paradox is that accepting the diagnosis and engaging in treatment is the very thing that will give your partner the best chance of living their life to its fullest. The longer they delay effectively managing their illness, the more it will disrupt their life.

My hope is that reading this book will help you understand the dilemma your partner faces when it comes to engaging in treatment. It's clear what you can do to support them, but it's also hard: You must sit with them in their ambivalence. Instead of pushing them with your conviction that they need treatment, you must create space to allow them to move of their own accord.

So, yes, express your opinion and observe that there are limits to what you are willing to tolerate. Recognize, however, that validating your partner's dilemma around treatment will enable them to join forces with you. Let them know you are at their side, but let them be the one to move forward. If you push them toward treatment, they're likely to dig in their heels, as if they need to defend something you want to take away.

As you continue to talk with them over time about treatment, here are a few principles to guide you:

- Be encouraging, loving, accepting, and respectful.

- Seek support from a therapist, friend, or support group if you need help with your own doubts and sense of defeat; sharing hopelessness about your partner's ability to make progress won't help either of you.

- Adjust your expectations and provide plenty of positive feedback for even the smallest steps forward.

- Convey that you see their struggle and encourage them with statements like "I know this is incredibly hard . . . I know you can do it."

- Be humble and gentle in sharing your opinion, acknowledging you may be wrong while insisting on your right to disagree.

If you and your partner can't reach an agreement about whether they should engage in treatment, seek common ground on overall values you share for your relationship. Perhaps you have a shared commitment to act with respect toward each other, to make each other feel good, to meet each other's needs in particular ways, or to take care of your children in a certain fashion. Starting with a statement of common values can help you reapproach the topic of treatment. That is, if your partner isn't living in line with your shared values, maybe they need some support figuring out how to do so. If they feel you're not living up to your end, maybe a therapist can help them get what they need from you and others.

Your partner's choices about treatment don't only affect them. You are involved, one way or the other. You care about their well-being, but you also must stand up for your own well-being and fight for the health of your relationship. Your partner's mental health condition impacts all these things.

It is from this perspective that, whether or not your partner wants to see their bipolar disorder as something that is managed in the context of your relationship, you can insist that they do. Their diagnosis is part of your life, and it's okay to have your own limits. You are allowed to speak up when you are uncomfortable and ask for what you need. You are allowed to take actions they don't like if, in your judgment, that is the right thing to do. In fact, you owe it to yourself. You can't control their response. They may respond negatively, and they may even leave. The alternative, however, is to sacrifice your own needs and self-respect to keep them close no matter what. This doesn't do anyone any good.

If you're uncomfortable because your partner does not have a therapist or psychiatrist they are working with, you should tell them that you are uncomfortable with this arrangement. This may be enough to get them into treatment, as they may be willing to do it for you. If what they're doing is crossing a line for you, then let them know they must alter their behavior if they want you to stay in the relationship.

You will have to decide for yourself what you can and can't live with. (We'll go into detail on how to observe your limits and set boundaries in chapter 7.) Some things will be nonnegotiable for you, and I recommend you think seriously about whether your partner's engagement in treatment should be one of them.

In Real Life

When Ekon shared his observation with Janice that it seemed like she couldn't sit still, she brushed him off. Now Janice has been up late three nights in a row, and she's starting to get that "wild look" in her eyes. She got angry when Ekon asked if she had stopped taking her meds. Despite their agreement that Ekon wouldn't check Janice's pillbox and Janice wouldn't lie about her meds, Ekon checks anyway. Sure enough, Janice has been out of meds for over a month.

Talk About It

If you relate to the dilemma above, here are some ways you can follow up with your partner regarding your concerns:

- "You said you wouldn't stop taking your meds, but you have. What's going on?"

- "I understand that I've violated your trust, and you have violated mine. I think we both want to trust each other, so what can we do about this?"

- "We've talked before about how you don't want to scare me. It's not you I'm scared of, it's the bipolar disorder, and I'm scared right now. I'm sorry if this makes you mad, but I'm asking you to call the doctor."

- "I respect your decisions about what's right for you. Remember what I said when you didn't think you needed the meds anymore? I said it was okay, but you agreed to see a psychiatrist if I thought you might be agitated or depressed. I'm going to hold you to that."

Write It Down

Take time to try to understand your partner's thoughts and feelings about treatment. If they are or have been conflicted, try to understand why that might make sense. In your journal, make a list of the pros and cons of treatment and medication from your partner's point of view. If their ambivalence still doesn't make sense, jot down some open-ended, nonjudgmental questions you might ask to understand their reasons for resisting treatment. For example, "Do you feel conflicted about whether or not to engage in treatment?"

What to Do If Your Partner Is Suicidal or Self-Harming

People with bipolar disorder are 20 to 30 times more likely to commit suicide than the general population. This will be less likely, and less frightening, if you and your partner take steps to manage the risk.

One helpful step is to talk with your partner about suicidal thoughts in advance. You can tell them you know these thoughts are not abnormal or uncommon. You can tell them that you don't judge them if they've had them and that you'd like them to tell you if they do. You can ask if your partner has created a "safety plan" with their therapist or psychiatrist, which will lay out how your partner will handle thoughts of suicide or self-harm. It is your partner's responsibility, hopefully with the help of a mental health provider, to keep themselves safe. You should never agree to play the role of stopping them from hurting themselves, and your partner should never ask you to. Their plan must include what they will do if you aren't there or aren't willing or able to help.

You can ask what role, if any, your partner wants you to play in their safety plan (and consider whether you're willing to play that role). If you are worried, ask if they would invite you to part of their session with a therapist or psychiatrist to discuss this. It will give you some comfort to have the name and phone number of their providers, and you must insist on having them if you are part of your partner's plan to stay safe.

If you need to assess the severity of your partner's suicidal thoughts, the most crucial questions to ask are whether your partner has thought about a specific way of killing them-selves and, if so, whether they have easy access to what they would need to carry out their plan. If the answer to either question is yes, they should not be left alone until they talk with a mental health professional. If you're worried for your partner's safety, cannot reach their provider, and aren't sure what to do, you can always call the National Suicide Prevention Lifeline (24/7, 365 days per year: 1-800-273-8255 or 1-800-SUICIDE); call 911; or, if you can do so safely, take your partner to an emergency room. If you find they have already taken action to kill themselves, call 911 and request immedi-ate medical assistance.

If your partner is self-harming (cutting, burning, hitting themselves, etc.), they may be doing this to manage their emotions, not because they have a wish to die. Even so, this is a serious sign that they need to be in treatment. Tell them you are not comfortable with this and insist that they see a mental health professional.

Facing a partner who is threatening to harm themselves is difficult, painful, and traumatic. It will create a shocking mix of emotions, including fear, anger, sadness, guilt, and numb-ness. If they blame or otherwise implicate you, this is unfair and abusive. Remember, no matter what you feel or what your partner says, it is not your job to stop them from hurting themselves and it is not your fault if they do.

Take a Mindful Minute

It's hard to think about your partner not getting the help they need. While it helps to know some of the ways you can support them, so many potential challenges and realities are beyond your control. But remember that your partner is not fragile—they have found what it takes to keep going, despite their challenges.

Set a timer for two minutes. Close your eyes and think about your partner's strengths, all the ways they've shown their resilience, and their ability to overcome adversity and stand on their own two feet. During this time, picture your partner rising to the occasion. Then, set the timer for another two minutes and think about all the ways their strengths help you when you need support. Imagine your partner during times they've given you what you needed.

If you see your partner resisting treatment or not taking care of themselves, you may worry that they won't "be okay" or that they can't provide what you need. You cannot control the future, and there is only so much you can do to impact it. Remembering the strengths your partner brings can help you let go of your worries when they are unhelpful. It can also help you appreciate your partner's presence in your life, even when their bipolar disorder makes things hard.

Chapter 4

Finding the Right Treatment

The primary treatments for bipolar disorder are medication, psychotherapy (therapy or counseling), education, and support groups. Within these categories are a dizzying number of options. This can be overwhelming, but it also means that if one treatment doesn't work, there are others to try. With so many options, bipolar disorder calls for recommendations from an experienced mental health practitioner who stays up-to-date on developments in the field.

This chapter is a brief introduction to the most effective medications and treatment options commonly used for bipolar disorder. Understanding the options will help you support your partner as they navigate treatment.

This chapter *does not* constitute medical advice and is not meant to guide your partner's treatment choices. Only a qualified professional who has conducted an in-person evaluation can make informed treatment recommendations.

Medication 101

You will find all sorts of information and strongly held opinions about medications online and elsewhere. Because individual responses to medications vary, both in terms of benefits and side effects, such a variety of information and opinions can be unhelpful. Rather than looking into it yourself, encourage your partner to find a psychiatrist experienced with bipolar disorder who can guide their treatment. It can take a few weeks or more to arrange a first appointment, so this isn't something to wait on. Particularly in the case of mood elevation, a delay could lead to an emergency room visit, while an early call to your partner's established psychiatrist could prevent an episode.

Your partner may use medication to manage their bipolar disorder in two ways: as an intervention for acute episodes and as an ongoing treatment to maintain stability and prevent episodes. Successful management usually includes both strategies. It's hard to remember to take medication regularly; a pillbox can help your partner organize their medications so that they do not lose track of them.

Medications for bipolar disorder are typically prescribed by a psychiatrist (MD or DO) or a psychiatric nurse practitioner (PMHNP or PMHCNS). Because of bipolar disorder's unpredictability, your partner should be engaged (or established) with a psychiatrist on an ongoing basis. To "establish care," your partner will need to have an intake appointment with a psychiatrist. Doctors are unlikely to prescribe medicine without doing this initial assessment.

Successful management of bipolar disorder typically involves trying different medications over time to learn what works best. Some will work better than others and some may have side effects or risks, so your partner will have to weigh the pros and cons for any given drug. Eventually, your partner and their psychiatrist can develop medication strategies for the various scenarios they may encounter, including:

- Long-term stability
- Emerging depression
- Emerging hypomania
- Acute depression
- Acute hypomania
- Mania
- Psychotic features

The following section is a brief introduction to the main categories of medications used for bipolar disorder. Each category contains many different individual drugs; here I'll name a few of the most common brand names. In general, medications have both generic and brand names, and these can look quite different (for example, Zyprexa is the most commonly known brand of olanzapine). People typically refer to the drugs by their most common brand name, but in reality, pharmacies often provide generic formulations or other brands when filling prescriptions.

Again, the following descriptions are general overviews—specific recommendations, information, and comprehensive advice about risks, benefits, and alternatives should be sought from a prescribing physician.

Mood Stabilizers

Mood stabilizers are the central feature of most ongoing medication regimens for bipolar disorder. When functioning well, a mood stabilizer does just what it sounds like. Depending on the situation and the medication, a mood stabilizer can not only keep things steady once episodes are resolved but can also be used to treat acute mood episodes.

Lithium is a mood stabilizer that has been used the longest for treatment of bipolar disorder. It is also one of the most widely studied and supported drugs in all psychiatry. Lithium can treat acute mania and can also protect against both mood elevation and depression when a person's mood is stable. What's more, there is strong evidence showing a reduced risk of suicide with long-term use of lithium. Because lithium can put strain on the kidneys, use of this drug involves monitoring kidney function with a blood test every few months.

In the 1980s, doctors began treating bipolar disorder with anticonvulsant medications originally used to treat epilepsy. They found these to have a powerful mood-stabilizing effect, and doctors have used them more and more commonly to treat bipolar disorder. Some mood stabilizers work better against depression than mood elevation, or vice versa. Commonly used anticonvulsant mood stabilizers include Depakote, Lamictal, and Tegretol. There are a variety of side effects people may experience as a result of taking a mood stabilizer. Quite bothersome and even severe side effects are possible, but more commonly, people may experience side effects like nausea, dizziness, and hand tremors, all of which may get better over time.

Antipsychotics

Antipsychotic medications are unfortunately named because of the stigma and misunderstanding associated with the word *psychotic*. In bipolar disorder, antipsychotics are frequently used to treat mood elevation, whether or not psychosis is part of the picture. When facing a dangerously acute mania speeding out of control, antipsychotics are generally what's needed to slam a foot on the brakes. Antipsychotics can also help with agitation, insomnia, and anxiety. They can be used to treat depression and as ongoing mood stabilizers as well—they are multitalented! Common antipsychotic drugs include Seroquel, Risperdal, and Abilify.

Your partner may struggle to tolerate some of the side effects that can accompany antipsychotics. These include weight gain, problems with attention and memory, blurry vision, loss of libido and/or menstrual periods, and drowsiness. These drugs can also cause extrapyramidal symptoms (EPS) which impact motor function, such as involuntary tremors or muscular contractions, restlessness, and agitation. Most EPS are temporary short-term reactions, resolving once the medication is discontinued. One type of EPS, *tardive dyskinesia* (repetitive involuntary movements) is irreversible, though it generally emerges only after long-term use of an antipsychotic.

Antidepressants

Antidepressant medications (ADMs) are widely used to treat major depressive disorder (MDD). Psychiatrists use caution with ADMs when treating bipolar disorder because they pose a danger of overshooting their intended effect, turning a depressive episode into hypomania or mania. Not infrequently, bipolar disorder becomes apparent for the first time during (or may be caused by) treatment of a major depressive episode with an antidepressant.

Antidepressants were first developed in the 1950s and have vastly increased in number over the years. At this point, there are five classes of these drugs and roughly 30 different medications to choose from. The more recent ADMs benefit from milder side-effect profiles and a more nuanced array of choices. These include selective serotonin reuptake inhibitors (SSRIs) like Zoloft and Lexapro and serotonin-norepinephrine reuptake inhibitors (SNRIs) such as Cymbalta and Effexor. Some of these medications have additional benefits such as reducing anxiety or helping with sleep.

Starting an antidepressant takes time because, while side effects may come immediately (and often taper off), it generally takes two to four weeks for the benefits of the medication to show up. Similar delays can accompany adjustments in dosage. Despite these challenges, your partner's medication regimen may include an ADM if it is effective at pulling or keeping them out of acute depression.

Benzodiazepines

Benzodiazepines are powerful antianxiety drugs. You may have heard them referred to as "benzos" (Xanax, Ativan, and Klonopin are some well-known brand names). With bipolar disorder, these medications are frequently used as a short-term or use-as-needed option to treat agitation and difficulty sleeping. Because lack of sleep is a badly destabilizing factor in bipolar disorder, these interventions can be crucial.

These medications unfortunately carry the potential for addiction and abuse. They are fast-acting and provide powerful relief, but the effects wear off quickly and can leave a person wanting more. Regular use can create tolerance and dependence, and stopping all at once can be dangerous. In some situations, however, psychiatrists may prescribe benzodiazepines for regular use.

Other Treatments

The following treatments are either relatively new or controversial and should not be tried without a doctor's advice. Nonetheless, your partner may come across these treatments and decide to try one or more, so they warrant mention here.

Bright light therapy (BLT): This therapy involves pre-scribed exposure to light. This is frequently done using a full-spectrum lamp, but natural sunlight, when available, may also be used. Studies have proven this effective in treating seasonal depression (a subtype of unipolar depression in which the fall/winter months regularly bring depressed mood). Conflicting evidence exists regarding BLT's effectiveness in treating bipolar disorder. Light exposure creates chemical changes in the brain and, like any treatment, should be used in consultation with a psychiatrist.

Electroconvulsive therapy (ECT): Stigmatized by the 1975 movie *One Flew Over the Cuckoo's Nest*, the use of ECT has grown again in the past decade as psychiatrists have been willing and able to challenge its stigma. This treatment is generally used only as a last resort because it can cause significant and sometimes permanent impacts to memory. It is, however, otherwise safe and effective and may be recommended for treatment-resistant depression (years-long acute depression that does not respond to other treatments).

Transcranial magnetic stimulation (TMS) and ketamine: TMS and ketamine are relatively new treatments for treatment-resistant depression. There is evidence behind their effectiveness in certain kinds of depression, but more studies are needed to establish their effectiveness in bipolar disorder. TMS is particularly attractive because it is noninvasive, does not involve medication, and has virtually no side effects. Treatment of depression with the drug ketamine, which is delivered during a series of doctor's visits, is still considered experimental at this time.

Complementary and alternative medicine (CAM): Even the most die-hard adherents of complementary and alternative medicine will agree that there is no clear scientific evidence supporting supplements or alternative remedies as a substitute for traditional medication for bipolar disorder. According to psychiatric CAM expert James Lake, MD, some evidence exists supporting supplemental treatments, including branched-chain amino acid drinks, magnesium, omega-3 fatty acids, and N-acetylcysteine (NAC). Your partner should consult with a psychiatrist before trying any supplemental treatments.

In Real Life

"So how did it go?" Jen asked Jin after he returned from the psychiatrist appointment he'd set up to help with his depression. "She said I have bipolar disorder and I have to take medication for the rest of my life." He put his head in his hands. "I thought she would just give me some Prozac. Now she's talking about so many different options and putting me on all this stuff I've never even heard of." After validating Jin's feelings of being overwhelmed, Jen offered to help him start by sorting through his new medications and writing them down.

Write It Down

Taking medication involves so many variables that it can quickly become confusing. You can ask your partner if they'd like your help by making two charts, which I recommend keeping electronically and physically so they can be easily accessed when consulting with a doctor.

One chart should be kept up-to-date with the medications your partner is currently taking—including the prescription (dosage and timing) and any notes such as dates of prescription changes, effects noticed, times when doses were missed, etc. The second chart is a historical record of the various medications your partner has tried. This should include as much detail as they can remember about when they took it and what effects it had. They can build from there with new medication for future reference.

Medication Challenges

Few people with bipolar disorder find it easy to start medication and stay on it as prescribed. Both positive and negative effects of medications are difficult for a doctor to predict. Side effects range from bothersome to intolerable. With so many options and none of them perfect, people end up trying multiple drugs with their psychiatrist in search of what works best. All the trial and error may end up making your partner feel "like a guinea pig." It can take years to find the best combination of medicines, and lifelong stability is rarely achieved on the first try. Even with the optimal "cocktail," there still may be some side effects.

People are generally motivated to take medication as prescribed during and following an acute mood episode. As the episode becomes a distant memory, they often lose their motivation or become convinced they no longer need medication and stop taking it. Ironically, the longer a period of stability with medication goes on, the more tempting it becomes to believe one can be stable without it. Given all the challenges of medication, who wouldn't want to hope or believe they shouldn't take it?

Your partner might adjust their medication on their own; they may increase or decrease doses, drop one medication, restart another, or stop altogether, without consulting their psychiatrist. In medical jargon, this means they are being *noncompliant* with their doctor's recommendations. The thing is, if your partner is taking matters into their own hands, it's not because they are trying to be difficult. They are trying to exert some control over how the drugs make them feel. Judging them for this is unfair and counterproductive.

If your partner fears disapproval from their psychiatrist, they might make impactful changes without telling them. Fear of disapproval may cause them to hide it from you as well. Unfortunately, stopping or changing medications against a doctor's recommendations and lying about what they're doing is one of the surest ways for your partner to self-sabotage when managing their bipolar disorder. This is why it's crucial that your partner find a psychiatrist with whom they feel comfortable. They should do their best to be honest about what's working, what's not, and what they are actually doing with regard to their medicines and other relevant lifestyle factors.

Even with the best psychiatrist, your partner may still find the relationship difficult. The psychiatrists I know are well-trained, knowledgeable, and caring people who are dedicated to easing emotional suffering. They took on two extra years of training following medical school because they wanted this to be their specialty. Unfortunately, many patients feel that their psychiatrist doesn't really care about or understand them, but this is actually a systemic problem. While a few psychiatrists work in private practice, most do not, and they are therefore limited in the time allotted to meet with their patients. This can make the relationship less productive than either the doctor or your partner desires, because there just isn't enough time to discuss decisions or answer questions.

Some argue that any research supporting medication is suspect because it has generally been funded by pharmaceutical companies. It's true that corporate funding has an impact on what research gets done, and we shouldn't trust everything that's touted as "research-supported" or "evidence-based." These claims should be independently evaluated with a critical eye. That said, we shouldn't throw out scientific consensus altogether. The smart thing to do is regard the research critically, not ignore it. The simple fact is that there are no peer-reviewed studies supporting long-term management of bipolar disorder without medication.

All of this can be discouraging, I know. Living with bipolar disorder is not for the faint of heart. You can help your partner by encouraging them to advocate for themselves. If they didn't get all their questions answered during their appointment with their psychiatrist, encourage them to request a follow-up phone call or to email their doctor if they can. Help them prepare for their appointments ahead of time by making notes about what to report and the questions they have. Ask them to be honest with themselves and their doctor about their willingness to continue with the medications they're taking and about any substances they're using. The doctor can only figure out how best to help them if they know what your partner is putting into their body.

You can also help by sharing some of the perspectives I've discussed here. Give your partner positive feedback about the ways they've worked hard to engage in treatment and validate that doing this is difficult. Let them know you understand that the mountain they must climb is daunting, that you understand why they sometimes slip and fall, and that you are still right there with them. Encourage them to be honest with you when it's hard to stick with medication plans, and assure them you won't judge.

In Real Life

Trish was outside humming and sketching flowers in the garden, feeling more like herself than she's been in months. "You seem so happy today, sweetie," said Darnell. Trish smiles and says, "Well, I know you won't approve, but I've been tinkering with my meds." Darnell raises an eyebrow, but checks himself. "Okay, well just keep track of what you're doing, okay? We'll write it down later tonight, and you can tell Dr. Williams so she can keep track, too."

Effective Therapeutic Treatments

While all the research points to lifelong medication as the most important treatment for bipolar disorder, there is strong evidence that psychotherapy makes a difference as well. You can help your partner get informed about the different kinds of therapy available. Like medication, there are many choices. Some psychiatrists provide therapy in addition to prescribing medication. This can be the ideal treatment setup because of its holistic and integrated nature, but it is typically more expensive than having a separate psychiatrist and therapist.

In this section, we'll look at some of the primary evidence-based therapies for bipolar disorder. "Evidence-based" treatment means that studies have shown the treatment to be effective at decreasing symptoms or improving certain outcomes. This kind of research matters to health insurance companies, which must determine which treatments they will pay for. Regardless of methodology, though, what's most important is how your partner feels about their relationship with their therapist.

Encourage your partner to try different therapists, if necessary, until they find one they like. The best way to find a therapist is through word of mouth, particularly the recommendations of other health-care or wellness professionals your partner trusts. A number of online services can help as well (see the Resources section on page 160 for more information).

Finally, whether or not your partner seeks one of the specific therapies described here, they may benefit from traditional "talk therapy," which is more generally supportive, or insight-oriented therapy. This approach is less about behavioral change and more about having time and space to reflect on oneself with the support of a professional. A diagnosis of bipolar disorder may represent a radical challenge to your partner's identity, and this kind of reflective space may help them make sense of it all. Most therapists these days have an integrative theoretical orientation, which means they will combine a variety of approaches to meet your partner's needs.

Psychoeducation

The non-medication intervention for bipolar disorder most clearly supported by research is *psychoeducation*. This simply means providing information about a mental health condition. It puts the information needed for insight, diagnosis, and treatment planning into your partner's hands, where it belongs. It's a great advantage if your partner can find a therapist experienced with bipolar disorder, because they can provide this important component. Psychoeducation can also be gained from books (like this one) and from groups or classes, as long as the sources are reputable (be skeptical of what you find on the internet).

Cognitive Behavioral Therapy (CBT)

Cognitive behavioral therapy (CBT) describes a broad approach that can be applied to many conditions. CBT is a practical, structured therapy that focuses on changing the way we behave and think in the present. CBT spends little time investigating the past or the deep inner workings of the self. It is collaborative, active, and goal-focused, with homework often assigned between sessions.

CBT for bipolar disorder will include psychoeducation and support to help your partner cultivate behaviors that facilitate their wellness and stability. It may teach new coping skills to deal with stress or help with relationships. It could involve helping your partner stay committed to taking their medication or remember to take it. CBT can also address unhelpful thinking patterns. If your partner is depressed and withdrawn, CBT could help them find the motivation and energy to reactivate and reengage. In general, a CBT therapist will look for what your partner is doing that might be getting in the way of their goals and then help them change those behaviors.

Dialectical Behavior Therapy (DBT)

Dialectical behavior therapy (DBT) utilizes CBT's change-focused strategies but balances them with the "acceptance"-based strategies of distress tolerance and mindfulness. DBT develops emotion-regulation skills, cultivating awareness in the midst of strong emotions and the ability to respond to them mindfully rather than react impulsively. DBT is based on the principle that learned, habitual behaviors can be unlearned and new habits can be formed, but only through repetition and practice. The structure of DBT supports this practice by teaching new skills or mindful choices.

While many therapists incorporate some DBT skills in the psychotherapy they provide, comprehensive DBT is an intensive, yearlong therapy. This could be recommended if your partner's long-standing patterns, even when stable, interfere with their ability to function or manage their bipolar disorder.

Family-Focused Therapy (FFT)

Family-focused therapy (FFT) will include anyone living with your partner or otherwise serving as a caregiver. If you have children, they may also be included. FFT is time-limited and generally delivered along with medication following a mood episode. This therapy proceeds from the perspective that bipolar disorder operates within a social context and that its course is impacted by the way your partner and their support system work together to cope with the illness. Doing FFT with your partner might help you develop your shared understanding of their bipolar disorder.

Interpersonal and Social Rhythm Therapy (IPSRT)

Interpersonal and social rhythm therapy (IPSRT) combines two basic kinds of therapy. The therapist will help your partner actively address interpersonal issues that are contributing to their depression. At the same time, they can use an innovative set of concrete tools to help your partner link their schedule to interactions with other people. This can help your partner establish a regular schedule and stable sleep regimen, which is intimately related to success in managing bipolar disorder.

In Real Life

Rafi rolled his eyes. "I've been to therapy before and talked all about my mother, and this is not what I need right now. I'm already taking a million meds, isn't that enough?" Justina responded, "I totally get that, but I've been learning about different kinds of therapy that are about the present, where you do homework and gain tools and skills, and you might only need to go for a few months."

Talk About It

Having read this section, you now know more than most about the different kinds of therapy choices specific to bipolar disorder. You may want to share this knowledge with your partner, especially if they don't have a therapist or don't like the one they have.

If your partner already has a therapist they're happy with, they may not need this information, so tread lightly. You don't want them to feel like you're criticizing the work they're already doing. As always, if you want to bring up the topic or share information, first make sure they're open to it. Let them know you've been doing some reading about bipolar disorder and have learned about some different kinds of therapy (or one in particular, if you like). Then, instead of telling your partner about these therapies, ask if they have heard of them. As always, make sure they know you are not trying to control them or tell them what to do.

If your partner isn't seeing a therapist and indicates that they might like to, ask if they'd like help taking the next step. If your partner is depressed, it may be especially hard for them to handle the logistics of getting a therapist. You can offer to do some research and present them with some therapists to consider or even set them up with some initial phone consultations.

Using Support Groups

Peer support groups are usually free and can play an integral role in managing bipolar disorder. Like therapy, they provide a supportive place where your partner can share their experiences. However, in a support group, your partner can connect with others who have similar struggles. It helps to feel that they're not alone and this can also counteract any shame they're feeling that could interfere with their being honest with you, their providers, and themselves.

Talking to others who share their diagnosis can help your partner process the identity challenges that come with it. They can learn from others' experiences and receive encouragement to stay engaged in treatment. They also have the chance to provide validation and support to other members of the group, which can feel good in and of itself. This feedback loop represents the power of community.

Support groups can play a key role in helping your partner monitor their mood by providing communal support and knowledge around how important this is and how to do it. A regular support group meeting can also help establish structure in the week. Moreover, attending a support group regularly by setting aside time to participate reflects your partner's willingness to focus on staying well. Information on how to find a support group is included in the Resources section at the end of this book (page 160).

Hospitalization and Higher Levels of Care

If your partner has an acute mood episode, more intensive short-term treatment may be warranted. In the most severe cases, they may need to be hospitalized. If you call 911 or your partner otherwise encounters first responders, including the police, they will be assessed for risk. If there are indicators that they may be an imminent danger to others or to themselves or if they are unable to provide for their own basic needs, such as food or shelter, first responders will take them to an emergency room, whether or not your partner agrees.

Unfortunately, an encounter with law enforcement may escalate your partner's symptoms. While police officers have been better trained to cope with mental health crises in recent years, their overall training focuses more on the use of force when faced with dangerous situations. This approach may not be helpful if your partner is in crisis and unable to think or respond rationally. You can play a crucial role with a 911 dispatcher and first responders on the scene: Tell them that your partner is suffering from a mental health crisis and give them a reasonable assessment of the danger your partner poses. They will approach the situation more calmly if they know your partner is unarmed, has no history of violence, or isn't in immediate danger. Tell them anything you know about what will calm or upset your partner.

Your local infrastructure may include a mobile crisis unit. These are first responders who are specifically trained to work with mental health crises and have additional training that can help them assess and de-escalate a tense situation with your partner. If appropriate, instead of hospitalizing your partner, they may work with them to make a plan to keep themselves safe until they can be seen in an outpatient setting.

You may ask a 911 dispatcher if they can arrange for a mobile crisis unit to respond, but they may send the police anyway. Mobile crisis units typically have their own fast-response phone number, but they may not be available around the clock. It is worth doing the research in advance (by looking online or calling your local police department's nonemergency number) so you will know how to contact them if need be.

Whether your partner is taken to an emergency room, goes on their own, or goes voluntarily with you, they will probably be placed on a temporary involuntary hold. If this occurs, they may not be allowed to leave the facility for 48 to 72 hours (depending on state law) and will be released only once it's been determined they are not a danger to themselves or others. Doctors in the emergency room can also transfer patients to an inpatient psychiatric ward, where they can be held longer, until the doctors are sure they can stay safe. Hospitalizations can be difficult, even traumatic, if your partner is held against their will, but they do ensure safety. They are also the quickest and sometimes the only way to get the medication your partner needs if they are suffering from full-blown mania.

There are also voluntary options for intensive care that can prevent hospitalization. From least to most intensive, these "higher levels of care" include intensive outpatient programs (IOP), partial hospitalization programs (PHP), residential programs, and short-term crisis residential programs. Length of treatment varies, typically between two weeks and three months. IOPs and PHPs are outpatient, so your partner can continue to live at home and go to the treatment environment for some portion of the day. All of these settings typically include medication management, as well as individual and group therapy.

Take a Mindful Minute

Learning about all of these various options, potential side effects, and investments of time and money can be mentally exhausting and stressful. Having delved into so much specific information in this chapter, this is a good time to step back from the trees and remind yourself of the forest. Why are you doing all of this work? What are your hopes? Your fears? What matters most to you and why?

Take a moment to respond to these questions in your journal. Journaling is a great self-care practice to process what you're going through and recenter on what's important to you. Writing down what you're stressed about can help you get it out and then "put the stress away" when you close the journal. It is also helpful to journal about things you are grateful for—even something as simple as a beautiful flower you noticed or a friendly smile from a stranger. Notice these things, both big and small, throughout the day and write them down later. Getting in touch with gratitude on a daily basis can do wonders for the spirit.

Chapter 5

Managing Bipolar Disorder Together

Supporting a partner with bipolar disorder is not a bystander activity. Bipolar disorder is a lifelong condition, and while there is no "cure," the condition responds positively and dramatically to active management. Remember, you and your partner are not powerless. They are the one with the official diagnosis, but the condition is profoundly social: Relationships impact the course of bipolar disorder, and vice versa, in dynamic and powerful ways. In this chapter, we'll look at how to join your partner in being proactive, thereby reducing vulnerability, building strength, and heading off episodes before they spiral out of control. You'll learn practical strategies to help you face adversity as a team, a challenge that can bring you and your partner closer together.

Warning Signs and Triggers

Early intervention is the key to preventing mood episodes. The earlier the intervention, the better the chance of avoiding the episode altogether, or at least reducing its severity. Because episodes emerge over time, it is possible to notice them early; however, the symptoms are also easy to overlook in the beginning. Essentially, successful management means learning how to notice and respond to emerging episodes before they become full-blown.

Even if it seems this way sometimes, mood episodes don't come out of nowhere. They are generally triggered by some kind of stress. When I say *stress*, I mean any type of impact to the system. The triggers don't have to be obviously negative or upsetting—getting a promotion or even falling in love might kick off an episode.

In life, stress is unavoidable. Stressful situations can occur anywhere. Triggers may result from onetime events or from the accumulated wear and tear of daily life, such as a difficult work environment, increased commitments, financial stress, or other anxiety-producing situations. Most likely, your partner's triggers are a combination of multiple stressors specific to their situation. Learning their specific triggers will go a long way toward preventing mood episodes.

We tend to think of stress as external, but impactful changes in the body's internal systems can be major triggers for mood episodes. The use of mood-altering substances such as alcohol, cannabis, caffeine, illegal drugs, and some prescription drugs is a common trigger. These can kick off episodes even if your partner's level of use wouldn't generally be considered substance abuse. Making medication changes without consulting a psychiatrist creates internal impacts that are also common episode triggers. Hormonal changes, changes in exercise intensity, and health-related conditions can all create internal conditions with stressful impacts on the body.

One of the most dangerous triggers for someone with bipolar disorder is a sudden disturbance in sleep, such as traversing time zones, pulling all-nighters, or working a night shift. Even changes in daylight related to the seasons can trigger mood episodes. Since changing sleep patterns are both a common trigger for and also a symptom of mood episodes, your partner's sleep habits/schedule is one of the most useful things for you and/or your partner to monitor and track on a daily basis.

Like sleep, activity levels and appetite can be monitored and tracked to catch episodes early: Increased or decreased activity can start as a mild symptom but then trigger the worsening of an episode. The same is true for changes in appetite or amount of food consumed. Along with sleep, energy, activity, and appetite, there may be subtler changes, such as changes in grooming habits or your partner's willing-ness to do certain activities.

By talking with your partner, you can learn how to better understand and identify the early warning signs of their symptoms. Your partner may already know what these are, so asking them what they've noticed will be your first step. As an outside observer, you will most likely notice some signs that your partner doesn't, which you should bring to their attention only *after* you've discussed doing so and your part-ner agrees.

You and your partner can also develop the ability to anticipate times when you'll need to be more watchful as a team. For instance, you may learn that potential triggers pop up when your partner is preparing for a business trip. Or that, if there is a party coming up, you'll want to be watchful for more frequent partying in the weeks that follow. If your partner's depression often comes with the fall and winter, you can become more vigilant ahead of time in August.

Another way to support your partner is to help them better manage their stress. Think about the ways you cope with stress—you'll probably find that some are more helpful than others. With your partner, identify their best coping strategies for stress. These could be anything from intense exercise to calling a family member or using active problem-solving. If you know what works for them, you can remind them to do it when they are stressed. Supporting your partner in a regular routine that keeps stress low—such as meditation, a recreational sports league, or time with friends—will be the best defense against the normal stressors your partner is bound to encounter.

In Real Life

Mimi and Chad have had a terrible year, culminating with Chad's layoff from work. Now that he's started his new job, Chad is finally his old cheerful self. But his after-work happy hours are becoming more frequent, and he's been staying up later once he comes home. Mimi doesn't want to rain on Chad's parade, but she's glad they've talked about how important it is for her to speak up—and for Chad to listen—when she sees a warning sign like increased drinking or getting by just fine on less sleep.

Talk About It

It's important to talk with your partner about their personal warning signs and triggers. They may have already learned what tends to trigger their episodes, so the best thing to do is to ask them. Conversely, they may not be aware of having triggers or what they are.

Reflecting on this together can help you support your partner when the triggers arise or help them avoid the triggers altogether. Find a time when you are both relaxed and feeling good to ask the following questions:

- "How do you know when an episode is coming on?"

- "Is it ever hard for you to recognize?"

- "If I notice [fill in the blank], would it be all right for me to let you know? What's the best way to do that?"

- "Is there anything I can do to help you avoid the triggers?"

Your Partner's Action Plan

So, what does a good action plan look like? We've worked through the beginnings of one: observing and identifying triggers and early warning signs. The rest of the plan will pair observations with actions, such as when to call a doctor or when to start closely tracking sleep patterns. It will also include protective actions and behaviors that can prevent a mood episode from emerging in the first place. The best kind of plan is written down and kept in both electronic and physical forms, where it is easily accessible to you, your partner, and the rest of their support team. You might even put a copy on your fridge.

Creating a good action plan may take some time and involve more than one difficult experience, so think of it as a work in progress. You may be looking forward to my laying out a series of steps for you to take if you think your partner is having a mood episode. Maybe you'd like a foolproof plan to make episodes go away as quickly as possible or to make sure they never happen again. If you don't have the right plan, you'll feel helpless, and you don't want to feel helpless in the face of bipolar disorder. You want a plan to stop bad things from happening!

I wish I could offer you that plan. I will certainly suggest some things you can do, but ultimately this isn't about *your* plan. Your partner is running the show when it comes to the behaviors that most affect their illness. They are the only one who can make their plan for prevention, monitoring, and intervention, and it has to work for them.

The most important interventions are steps your partner will have to take, and those steps are difficult, especially if they are having a mood episode and may no longer think they need to take them. This is why it will be helpful if they are willing to write the plan down and share it with you. This is the only way both of you can know for sure that the plan is being followed.

If you are to be actively involved in your partner's plan, they must want to make the plan with you and be willing to accept your help following it. If they can let you in like this, your relationship will thrive, but it's not a small ask for you to make; it will be hard for them to let you be a part of their struggle. For this reason, the task that lies ahead for you doesn't come down to a series of action steps. Instead of focusing on what *you* can do, think more about how you can *be* with your partner. Making and sticking with their plan will be exceedingly difficult for them. If you see them fall or falter, your job is to be a good coach.

According to the International Olympic Committee, being a coach means being "positive, enthusiastic, supportive, trusting, focused, goal-oriented, knowledgeable, observant, respectful, patient, and a clear communicator." What you can do is this:

- Recognize your partner's efforts with positive reinforcement.

- Encourage them: "I know you can do it!"

- Express appreciation that they are trying and doing the best they can.

- Be curious about your partner's experience by asking how they're doing and feeling.

- Listen openly and do your best to understand.

- Accept and validate their perspective.

- Stay hopeful and positive, even when they can't.

There are a few concrete actions you can offer, but these will only help if your partner actively wants you to do them:

- Share your observations of shifts in their mood, energy, and activity.

- Provide or help them find the resources/time they need to engage in activities that are important to their wellness.

- Help them stay organized with regard to medication, treatment appointments, and important activities.

- Help them work with their doctors, reach out to their support network, or engage crisis services as needed.

It can be frustrating if your partner won't let you help as much as you would like, but providing unwanted forms of support just won't be effective. Your partner needs a plan of action that reflects *their* knowledge of what they need. Your interventions must be part of that plan. To learn how you can be most supportive, refer to your partner's plan of action.

If your partner doesn't already have a working plan in place and is interested in creating one, you can tell them about WRAP. The Wellness Recovery Action Plan (WRAP), developed in 1997 by Dr. Mary Ellen Copeland, is an evidence-based practice that provides a framework for your partner to make an action plan. Many versions of similar templates have since been developed and are widely available, including Dr. Copeland's most recent and comprehensive version, updated in 2018.

A WRAP plan incorporates the following principles:

- The plan is written by and for the person with bipolar disorder. They decide what's in it, and no one can tell them that they need one.

- They can change the plan whenever and however they want.

- They decide with whom they share it.

- It's not just a crisis plan, but rather a plan for daily living.

WRAP breaks your partner's plan into the following sections:

Wellness: Being well means something different for everyone. A plan begins by describing their well state. What does wellness mean to them? What are the specific markers that tell them they are well?

Recovery: Your partner is personally responsible for working on their wellness and recovering from past illnesses or episodes. They must learn, advocate for themselves, and build the support they need. Their hope lies in their ongoing self-empowerment.

Action: A good plan includes concrete actions and activities that help your partner feel better when their wellness is threatened. This can mean any number of things, from accessing their support network (perhaps you or their doctor) to going to sleep at a reasonable hour or taking their medication. Learning what works is an ongoing process your partner can go through with you or their therapist.

Plan: A WRAP plan is written down. It builds on strengths, reduces vulnerabilities, and tells your partner how to know when they're not feeling well and what to do.

For more information on creating a WRAP plan, you can order Dr. Copeland's version, which is listed in the Resources section (page 163).

Notice the framework for the support system in the WRAP plan. Your support is part of the recommended plan, but it is your partner's responsibility to build that support and design what it looks like. You can help them with their task by asking them what they need and telling them what you are willing and not willing to do.

All the advance teamwork you've done on identifying triggers is helpful here, because emerging mood episodes interfere with the capacity for insight. Your outside perspective allows you to ring the warning bell, and this can be a powerful help—if your partner wants it. The challenge comes when your partner wants to argue with you about your observations. The more you have written down together in advance, the clearer it will be for both of you that, even if your partner protests, you are following the plan your partner created.

In Real Life

Angel and Carlotta started consulting Carlotta's WRAP plan actively a few weeks ago when they noticed she was more irritable than usual, a warning sign for her hypomanic episodes. Carlotta's plan calls for daily meditation and monitoring sleep, which they began tracking in a journal. According to her plan, decreased sleep five days in a row signals that it's time for Carlotta to call her doctor for advice.

Write It Down

When your partner is stable, ask if they'd be willing to talk about (and even write down) the ways in which you can better support them in managing their bipolar disorder. Explain that you'll feel better if you have a plan in place, so you know what to do when a mood episode occurs and what support to provide. In expressing your desire to help, be sure to approach the conversation with humility and curiosity: Never assume you know what they will say or that you know best.

If your partner is resistant when you bring up the topic, emphasize that you're asking for something you really need, and what you need is not for them to listen to your opinions but rather for them to talk to you about their experience and their needs. For instance, you could say something like: "I keep getting the message that you've got it covered and don't want to talk about it, but this leaves me feeling alone. I know I have to trust you and that you know bipolar disorder better than I do, but I'm scared that I won't know what to do. If you could write it down for me in advance, then I can feel like, no matter what, we're in this together."

When your partner is ready, write down together when and how you will (or won't) intervene or offer your partner support. The more collaborative you can be in this process, the more effective the plan will be. Consider the following questions, and ask that your partner make their answers as specific as possible:

- "At what point should I intervene?"

- "What would be a good way for me to talk about my concerns?"

- "What is most helpful/productive for you to hear?"

- "What's the best way for me to be supportive?"

- "Would you like support with anything you want to do for self-care?"

- "Would you like help staying organized for treatment appointments or medication?"

- "When should we contact your treatment providers?"

- "What's the plan when a crisis occurs?"

Empathy and Patience

Even with an action plan in place and a commitment to treatment, getting better at managing bipolar disorder takes time and your partner is bound to stumble. It can be enormously difficult to maintain empathy and patience with a mood disorder, and you can't expect yourself to be perfect in this regard. Furthermore, your partner is accountable for their choices, especially those that affect their illness. When they make bad or irresponsible choices regarding their health and wellness, you have a right to be angry. It's crucial to remember two things:

- You are not responsible for your loved one's choices.

- Protecting them from consequences tends to be unhelpful.

A good question to ask yourself is, "Am I angry at my partner or is my anger more properly directed at the illness itself?"

Either way, strive to be empathetic and patient. Bipolar disorder is not only debilitating at times, it is invisible, misunderstood, and stigmatized. Part of your partner's suffering is a deep confusion, on both their part and the part of others, over how to interpret their actions. You or others might look at their choices and ask, "Why don't they just . . .?" This question is both unanswerable and unhelpful. Your partner did not choose to have bipolar disorder.

During an acute episode, your partner's ability to control their behavior is impaired. The illness attacks their insight and judgment, which are the very faculties we depend upon to make good choices. Instead of blaming them for not doing what they need to do, see that what they need to do is difficult and they are doing their best. Pointing fingers is inevitably destructive to your relationship because it creates a win-or-lose situation, where the only way forward is to fight.

Both you and your partner are doing the best you can with the information you have and the skills you have learned (even if it doesn't always feel that way), and you are both continuing to learn. This doesn't mean that actions don't have consequences, but giving yourself and your partner the benefit of the doubt can open up the doors of compassion.

Imagine what it would feel like for you to be unable to control or predict your emotions, your energy, or your ability to function. Imagine if your life depended on lifelong medication that didn't always work and the ability to adhere to a strictly balanced lifestyle. Imagine the shame and heartbreak you'd feel if, whenever you got sick, you alienated your friends and acted in ways you yourself would find abhorrent.

These realities are difficult to accept, and it's easy to feel hopeless. As hard as it is to hang in there, though, empathy and patience are necessary to keep you moving forward. This is a marathon, not a sprint, and it will often be two steps forward, one step back. Medication adjustments can be a never-ending process; episodes can happen despite every possible effort to prevent them, but your partner cannot give up—that will only put them back at square one. Help them stay engaged, keep learning together, and keep supporting each other.

In Real Life

The call comes at 2:00 a.m. from the ER. Shay hasn't been home for three days, and her pillbox shows she hasn't taken her meds in a week. Driving to the hospital, Randy is filled with anger and anxiety. Shay's latest spree has completely eroded their financial cushion. Outside the ER, Randy pauses to center himself, reminding himself that Shay didn't ask for this infernal illness; neither of them did. He takes a deep breath and enters her room: "Oh Shay, sweetheart, thank goodness you're all right."

Take a Mindful Minute

In this chapter, you learned how to start identifying triggers and how to get involved in your partner's action plan. Remember that this is a lifelong journey and it will take ongoing effort. You may even be at a point of exhaustion right now.

Life can often be so fast-paced that checking in with yourself and taking a mindful breath might be the last thing on your mind. It's especially important, though, to connect with yourself and your breath during times of intense transition.

Check in with yourself right now:

- What are you feeling in your body?

- What thoughts are going through your mind?

- What emotions are coming up for you?

Now, take three slow, deep breaths in through your nose and out through your mouth.

To remind yourself to breathe deeply throughout the day, try this: Whenever you are about to cross the threshold of a door, stop and pause for a moment to connect back to your breath. Notice any urges you have to skip or lose focus during these mindful moments and ask yourself, "Is there truly not a moment to spare for myself?" Remind yourself that there's always time to breathe.

Chapter 6

Keeping Yourself Sane

So far, we've covered a lot of the information necessary to understand bipolar disorder and how to support your partner. This is terrific! Perhaps you are even thinking that you've got this, no problem. This confidence in your capability is what we're after here. But when you feel that you and your partner have conquered bipolar disorder, though, you might be experiencing some denial. If so, then know that denial is a normal and healthy part of the process. Chances are, though, you have other feelings as well that need to be processed. In this chapter, you'll learn how to identify and acknowledge your feelings, seek support when you need it, and find time for yourself.

Acknowledge Your Emotions

Standing by someone with bipolar disorder means you may tend to focus solely on their emotional life. But *your* feelings are equally important to focus on as well.

Feelings are never right or wrong; they are complicated, natural responses to what is going on in your life. Strong feelings come with an impulse to do something. When we are angry, for instance, we want to attack; when afraid, we want to run. We try to stop ourselves from following counter-productive urges, but it can be hard. It helps to have some validation of our distressing feelings. When someone validates us, they name and acknowledge our feelings and verify that our feelings make sense, given our history, state of mind, and current situation.

Your partner won't always validate you (and when they don't, it hurts), so learning to validate yourself is important. Otherwise, you end up burying your feelings, which doesn't help. In the following sections, we'll go over some of the more common feelings you may experience, helping you make sense of them, validate them, and respond to them more effectively.

In Real Life

Shane is on her third drink at the bar, scrolling mindlessly through social media on her phone. She'll wait to go home until she's sure Victor's asleep. She's never told her friends about his grueling depressive episodes—too embarrassing—but she's stopped telling her parents when they happen, too. "He's fine," she'll say, even when she knows he's not. She's done trying to get him off the couch. Even when he cries now, she feels nothing. "Just get through the night," she tells herself. "Tomorrow I'll be back at the office, and I won't have to deal with this."

Anger

Impaired judgment is a symptom of mood episodes, but that doesn't make it any less infuriating if your partner betrays your trust, especially if it's happened before and you've told them how much it hurt you. You may feel anger around your partner's infidelity, excessive spending, substance use, or any other behavior that your partner lies about and hides. You will also feel anger if your partner attacks or threatens you, your children, or something you care about.

Anger is one of the most difficult feelings to manage, because its accompanying urge is to attack, which is rarely effective. If you're feeling angry with your partner, disengage from them long enough to calm yourself down. Losing your temper with them will only make things worse.

If you avoid conflict entirely, though, you won't improve the situation and may make matters worse. You are angry because your partner has threatened something you value. You will need to tell them in no uncertain terms that it's not okay and you don't want them to do it again. Otherwise, you will end up keeping your anger inside. Unexpressed anger will intensify, creating resentment, bitterness, emotional withdrawal, and passive-aggressive behavior. Worse, you may turn your anger against yourself, deciding that the hurt you experienced is your own fault. This leads to self-destructive thoughts and actions.

A good strategy, once you've calmed down, is to name your anger and share it calmly with your partner: "I felt angry when . . ." Stick to concrete and objective observations when describing your partner's actions. Focus on describing your feelings and the impact they had on you instead of arguing over what your partner actually did or meant to do. The conversation will be less likely to escalate into an argument over who caused what and more likely to remain a validation of your own feelings.

Frustration

Frustration can build into anger, but it's not the same. We feel frustrated when, despite our repeated efforts to address a problem, the problem keeps happening. Expressing frustration often begins with, "No matter how hard I try . . ." You may feel frustrated if you see your partner not taking good care of themselves or doing things you know can make their bipolar disorder worse, such as dropping out of treatment, frequent napping, misusing substances, overworking, withdrawing socially, or failing to maintain routines critical to their mental health.

Your partner's depressive episodes may be especially frustrating, because one of their symptoms may be loss of motivation. If you push them, it may not help, and you may feel guilty for not accepting that they don't feel well. If you don't push them, they may not push themselves. Meanwhile, you're watching as your partner makes things worse for themselves and for you.

Feeling frustrated often prompts us to problem-solve, as if we simply haven't found the right solution to what's bothering us. Before you keep problem-solving, though, stop to make sure you have properly identified the problem. If you've already tried everything you can to fix a problem, then maybe you're trying to fix the wrong problem.

Ask yourself if the problem is actually this: You continue to feel bothered by something that will never change. In this case, if you want to stop feeling frustrated, you will need to work on accepting reality or perhaps changing how you feel about it. If it's a weakness in your partner that frustrates you, look for the flip side. Most weaknesses come with strengths, and vice versa. If you can't identify a strength, try to find some humor in the situation. If you're frustrated because your partner keeps exhibiting behaviors that are unacceptable, this is different. The next chapter addresses what to do if your partner keeps crossing your boundaries.

Fear

Fear is an emotion that signals danger, such as a threat to ourselves or something important to us. Shocking and frightening things can happen during mood episodes. Your partner's behavior may become hardly recognizable. They may lose control in front of you, displaying rage or destructiveness or behaving recklessly in ways that endanger your safety and the safety of those around you. They may become suicidal (page 46 addresses ways you can respond if this occurs). In these situations, you will experience fear at the core of your being.

Whether or not your partner has exhibited behaviors like these before, you may fear that they will. You may fear they will repeat other disastrous things they've done in the past: perhaps losing their job, spending money they don't have, burning bridges in other relationships, etc. These affect fundamental elements of your own security because they erode your partner's ability to be there for you when you need them.

We use the word *anxiety* to describe a consuming or repetitive fear of what may happen. Both you and your partner will inevitably worry about a possible mood episode and all that could come with it. The two best ways to reduce anxiety are to:

- Increase certainty about what will happen by collecting more information.

- Take any steps you can to decrease the likelihood of a negative outcome.

Let's say you're worried about your financial security because your partner, who is depressed, keeps saying they're going to lose their job. Collecting information could mean getting a really good sense of your family's financial situation. If you cut your spending to bare essentials, exactly how long could you maintain your monthly budget without their income? Would your or your partner's family be able to help? Taking steps to increase safety could mean creating a contingency plan or doing whatever it takes to make sure your partner leaves for work on time.

If there's nothing more to do to increase certainty or make a meaningful impact on a future outcome, however, you must work to accept the uncertainty and spend less time worrying about it. The first thing is to observe and label it when it's happening: "This is an unhelpful worry." Practice self-compassion, recognizing that you're living with uncomfortable uncertainty. Once you've interrupted the worry, try something to soothe or distract yourself (page 33). If it's a big worry, you won't be able to put it out of your mind forever, but if you practice this sequence again and again, you'll get better at putting it out of your mind for the moment.

Hopelessness

If your partner's bipolar disorder causes frustration and anxiety over a long period, you may start to feel hopeless about your relationship. The bedfellow of depression, hopelessness is the feeling that comes with believing things will never get better: "They'll never change . . . ," "I can't do this . . . ," "We're doomed . . . ."

Learning to combat hopelessness is important, because the feeling is incompatible with a happy life. It's hard to manage this feeling, however, because it's tied to the thought that change is impossible. Hopelessness brings with it the urge to give up.

There are at least two productive approaches when you begin to feel this way. First, remind yourself that, while you can't change the past, you also can't know the future. Maybe your partner's bipolar disorder has been intolerable thus far—it's pushed you to your breaking point. But that doesn't mean things can't change. There are so many variables: You and your partner may get better at managing the condition, your partner and their psychiatrist may arrive at the right combination of medication, advances in medicine may improve treatment options, and circumstances may change for better or worse. Remind yourself that, while feeling hopeless is valid and understandable, the feeling will pass when you find hope for the future.

A second productive approach is to remind yourself that you are not powerless: You can (and do) make choices that affect the situation. Remember also that you are not trapped: Ending or changing the terms of your relationship are available choices, even if you may not like them. You may think you must either tolerate the intolerable or end the relationship. This is a false duality. Life presents many choices and many possible outcomes, not just two options.

Grief

In the development of any healthy, long-term relationship, discovering things that feel intolerable comes with the territory. The simple, boundless excitement of falling in love gives way to the complications of life. We discover more dimensions to our partner, not all of them attractive. On some level, every couple goes through the experience of losing some of their hopes and dreams for their life together. When we acknowledge these kinds of losses, we experience sadness and grief.

Grieving is healthy. Recognizing loss transforms hopelessness into sadness, and, while sadness doesn't feel good, it does allow you to move through it, rather than feeling trapped or stuck. It can be difficult to maintain a feeling of connection with your partner while you're working through the acceptance of disappointments in your relationship. Have patience. Many relationships make it through such rocky times and become more resilient as a result. Some don't make it, and that can be a healthy outcome, too. Regardless, while it does hurt, recognizing the heartbreaks and heartaches helps more than denying them.

Shame

When your partner is not stable, they may act in ways that are out of character for them and inconsistent with their personality. You may not feel proud of the way they are acting or you may feel bad about the ways you are responding. You may feel shame for staying with them. You may think that the difficulties in your relationship are all your fault or your partner may be giving you the message that they are. The shame that accompanies blame and anger is more properly directed at the condition, not each other.

While having bipolar disorder should not warrant shame, the shame you feel is an understandable result of misunderstanding and unjust stigma in society. You are doing your best in the context of loving a partner who suffers with a serious and confusing mental illness. Not everyone will understand this immediately. Unfortunately, the urge to "hide" that accompanies shame sometimes makes sense with regard to bipolar disorder: Your partner is right to think twice, for instance, before broadcasting their diagnosis to their professional community.

On a personal level, however, work against this shame. Don't hide the struggle from trusted friends and family members. Tell them about your experience and educate them as needed so they can be there for you. It is important to have people with whom you feel safe and supported, no matter what you are going through.

Love

Love is a huge and complex feeling, able to contain many other feelings and attached to a history of shared experiences. The urge that accompanies love is the desire to be close. This can express itself in many ways, of course, and your desire to understand and help your partner is one of them. Love can get you through the rocky times.

As you experience and process the more difficult feelings, it helps to make an active effort to stay connected with your love for your partner. This means taking a step back to look at the big picture, letting go of the trees for a moment to see the forest, and remembering what made you fall in love with your partner in the first place. Ensure you are making time for each other, spending time doing the things you love to do together, and keeping the channels of communication open. Let your partner know you are trying to make the relationship work for both of you.

At the same time, it is important to regard love rationally. Love is at the heart of our survival as a species, the glue that binds us together. Love creates our willingness to compromise and find common ground. This power can be destructive if it causes us to go too far in sacrificing our own needs. This can lead to codependency, where one person's extreme caretaking can reinforce the other person's dependency, and vice versa. (Codependency is discussed in more detail in chapter 7.)

In Real Life

Farah can't believe she'd been holding so much inside. Last night was particularly hard and, after Adil went to sleep, she sat down with the journal she had bought months ago but never started. She began writing, and pretty soon it all poured out—the fear, the frustration, the grief, the tears. She can't remember the last time she cried like that. This morning she feels spent but also open and free. It's important to keep opening up to herself, she thinks, and she decides to write in her journal at least once each weekend.

Seek Support

With bipolar disorder, intense feelings come with the territory, and it's important for you to have support. You can and should discuss your feelings with your partner, of course, but your partner's own feelings may lead them to be defensive in response. Whether or not that's the case, you need to find support from other sources as well. In this section, we'll discuss some of the ways you can reach out for help.

Family and Friends

Your family and friends know you best, but seeking help from them may be challenging. Some may have preconceived notions about bipolar disorder due to the associated stigma. If what you share is upsetting to them, you may find yourself taking care of their needs instead of the other way around. They may push you to act in ways that might make them feel better but don't make sense to you.

If your friends or family are supporting you in unsatisfying ways, think about what's missing and bring it up with them explicitly. They likely want to be supportive but they may not know what you need or understand that what they are doing is unhelpful. If you can explain it to them effectively, they are likely to try to respond and give you the kind of support you need.

Talk About It

Here are some scripts that might help communicate your needs to friends or family:

- "I'm going through something difficult and I need support. It's pretty complicated and hard to understand and you might find it upsetting, but would you be willing to try to listen without reacting immediately?"

- "I want to talk to you about this, but I'm afraid you'll leap to conclusions or tell me what to do."

- "That's an idea, thank you. I don't think I need help with problem-solving right now. What I really need from you is (fill in the blank)." (For example, "some comforting" or "just to know you're here for me no matter what" or "a hug.")

- "Bipolar disorder looks really different from person to person. It would help me if you understood it a bit better. Would you be willing to (fill in the blank)?" (For example, "read something about it" or "listen while I explain a bit.")

Therapy

No matter how well your friends and family support you, you can't ask them to be an objective third party. Your life and how you're doing impacts them. They may even be actively involved in the situation. A therapist can support you in many helpful ways, in part because the relationship is less compli-cated and completely focused on your needs.

Every psychotherapist is different, and there are many dif-ferent kinds of therapy. These days, therapists often have an "integrative" orientation, meaning they will pick and choose techniques to use based on your needs. When seeking a therapist, it's a good idea to try out more than one to get a feel for what you need and who will be a good fit for you.

One thing to consider is whether you're interested in explor-ing your own emotional responses, how they came to be, and why they are difficult to change. On the other hand, you may want primarily practical skills and tools to change present pat-terns, and this is important to mention upfront to a potential therapist. Here are a few helpful functions therapy may offer:

Basic support and stress relief. A therapist can provide a lis-tening ear and an outside perspective while you talk through what you're experiencing. This can provide relief, clarity, encouragement, and hope. A therapist may also help with self-care and other stress-relief techniques.

Communication skills, assertiveness, and boundary-setting. If this is your focus in individual therapy, it may be particu-larly helpful if your therapist has helped others whose loved ones struggle with mental illness. Couples or family therapy can be an effective way to address these issues.

Gaining insight. Insight-oriented or psychodynamic therapy can help by increasing your awareness of why and how you respond to the dynamics in your relationship. You may be able to learn new ways to respond or share your insights with your partner in helpful ways.

Processing trauma. If your relationship frequently triggers intense and overwhelming negative emotions in you, trauma-focused therapy may help you learn to stay grounded and heal from the effects of past trauma.

Support Groups

Whether or not you see a therapist, I recommend trying out a support group created for people whose loved ones have a mental illness. Support groups are generally free, and they offer a safe, nonjudgmental space where you don't have to feel alone with the struggle. You may also learn helpful strategies that you can easily implement. You may feel intimidated, embarrassed, or shy if you've never attended a support group before, but try to overcome your hesitation and just give it a try. If you don't feel like sharing yourself, it's totally fine in such a group to just quietly listen. You may also feel like talking about your experience, receiving supportive feedback, or asking specific questions. These are all great ways to use a support group.

Two organizations I recommend are the Depression and Bipolar Support Alliance (DBSA) and the National Alliance on Mental Illness (NAMI). See the Resources section (page 160) for these organizations' contact information.

Online Communities

Online communities offer support groups, family-to-family chat rooms, and specific suggestions for problem-solving and coping skills. The NAMI offers an innovative family-to-family program for free. This is a structured, research-supported, eight-session program conducted by NAMI-trained family members. Other online communities include the Bipolar Disorder Support Group and Bipolar, Schizophrenia, and Psychosis Support. See the Resources section (page 160) for contact information for these groups.

In Real Life

Antoine has been playing the caregiver role for Ryan and his bipolar disorder for years. He has always brushed off suggestions that he should have his own therapist, but the situation is starting to get to him. He doesn't like how angry and resentful he feels, and he always feels guilty for having these thoughts or not doing more. Antoine's been having trouble sleeping, and it's a struggle to concentrate at work. It's time he gets some support himself.

Find Some "Me" Time

Here you are reading this book when you might be otherwise taking care of important business or doing something fun. Bipolar disorder is probably taking up more space in your life than you'd like. It's important to make time for yourself. This is especially true if it feels like the combination of your relationship and your other responsibilities requires all of your attention, and there's not a moment to spare. If you are feeling this way, this may indicate that you are in danger of burning out. If you don't take care of your own needs, you will lose the ability to care for others. It's just as they say in the airline safety presentation: You must first put on your own oxygen mask before assisting others.

Attend to basic self-care: Engage in regular exercise, follow a healthy diet, and get enough sleep. There are precious few things you can do that will have a bigger impact on your own mental health. Another important aspect of "me" time is doing things that bring you pleasure and relief. Spending time on this is critical so that you will be rested, recharged, and able to refocus productively on your responsibilities.

Are there tasks you keep putting off that will make you feel good once they're no longer hanging over your head? Are there activities or hobbies you love but don't engage in anymore? What are some fun things you've been meaning to try?

Whatever actions these questions bring to mind for you, don't wait another moment or put it off another day. It's important to practice finding "me" time every day. Take a moment to walk around the block and absorb the fresh air. Even just a few minutes of outside time every day can positively impact your mental health.

Write It Down

Journaling is a great tool to discover what we need more of in our lives. In your journal, answer the following questions and take the steps necessary to prioritize yourself:

1. What kind of support do you need? Friends and family? Therapy? Support groups? "Me" time? Something else?

2. For each type of support you identify, write down some specific options for where you might find it.

3. For each option, write down the next step to take in making it a reality.

4. Pick one option and plan when you will take that step. Put it in your calendar.

5. The next time you feel overwhelmed and need support, stop trying to get things done and instead take a deep breath. Spend one minute writing down your next step toward self-care.

Take a Mindful Minute

In this chapter, you learned about recognizing your feelings, how to manage them, and ways to seek support. Gaining insight into hard feelings is helpful, but it also requires bringing those feelings to the surface. This can be emotionally painful. Knowing that support is available can be comforting, but thinking about reaching out for it may feel overwhelming.

Take time to refresh and rejuvenate by spending a few minutes engaging each of your senses in a way you find soothing. Your senses have a direct line to your nervous system and can skip over all your thoughts to directly relax your body. Each of the five senses is listed below along with a few suggestions. You can use these ideas or create your own. Set aside at least one minute for each sense to practice. (This technique is adapted from Marsha M. Linehan's *DBT Skills Training Handouts and Worksheets*.)

- **Sight:** Look at appealing artwork, watch a candle flame, or look at pictures of loved ones or animals

- **Hearing:** Play or listen to music, wind chimes, or the sounds of nature

- **Taste:** Savor a mint or hard candy, eat a crunchy fruit or vegetable, or enjoy some tea or hot chocolate

- **Touch:** Caress a soft blanket, take a bath or shower, or change into comfortable clothes

- **Smell:** Bake something, light incense, or smell a flower

This activity can be helpful anytime you need a break from a fast-paced day. Identify something soothing that you can have with you always, as well as something special for you to enjoy when you are at home.

Chapter 7

Keeping Yourself Safe

We generally end relationships with people who make us feel uncomfortable and unsafe. With your partner, however, everything may be good when they're stable, but some of their behaviors may cross the line for you if they're having a mood episode. Also, because bipolar disorder is a chronic health condition, it naturally pulls a partner into the role of permanent caregiver. If you have taken on this role even partially (especially if you are also a caregiver to others), it creates pressure for you to over-extend yourself or to excuse behaviors that really aren't okay. In this chapter, we'll discuss how to identify these issues and discuss them effectively with your partner.

Boundaries and Limits

We establish boundaries by asking for what we need and speaking up when we don't want to do something. Setting boundaries sounds simple and obvious, but in practice, it can be tricky. When it comes to intimate relationships, we want to be close to our partners and meet their needs. At the same time, we don't want to sacrifice our own needs or be too demanding. We may worry that asking for something or saying no will push us apart.

Setting boundaries can also feel slippery when behaviors are not extreme. A black-and-white approach may not capture the complexity involved. Dr. Marsha Linehan's concept of "observing limits" can be helpful here. Observing limits isn't about drawing a line; it's about taking ownership for what we need. Limits can be flexible, because our needs may change over time based on changing circumstances. We can learn to recognize our limits being pushed, and we can weigh what we are willing to do or tolerate at a given moment. We can check in with ourselves often and communicate clearly about what our limits are.

By observing, naming, and respecting your limits, you and your partner can together recognize and honor the truth of your relationship: No matter how close you are, no matter how much you care, you remain two separate people. You have different needs at different times, and these needs will sometimes conflict.

It seems like a paradox, but it's true: Acknowledging and naming the presence of conflict is actually the way to get through it successfully and without damaging your relationship. Sometimes partners in a relationship try to ignore conflict by neglecting one partner's needs in favor of the other's in a cycle called *codependency*.

In a codependent relationship, partners play complementary roles: the "Giver" and the "Taker." The Giver takes on the needs of the Taker as their own. The Taker gets used to being the top priority, comes to depend on it, and may be angry when the Giver fails to fulfill expectations. The Giver then feels compelled to anticipate and meet the Taker's needs, and grows resentful as they sacrifice their own. Both partners somehow believe the Taker cannot get by without the Giver's support. Deep down, they both feel scared and trapped, and both are responsible for perpetuating this cycle.

In a codependent relationship, the Giver may break down in protest from time to time, but guilt over not meeting the Taker's needs draws them back in. The Giver can also become an enabler, reinforcing the Taker's self-destructive behaviors by assuming responsibility for preventing them or by protecting the Taker from negative consequences.

Codependency isn't something people choose; it sneaks into a relationship. It's incredibly hard to avoid when one partner has a chronic illness like bipolar disorder. If your partner had the passing flu, for instance, putting their needs above your own for the moment makes sense. With a chronic condition, however, you must be vigilant not to let this be an unhealthy pattern. This will mean accepting that you can't always be there for your partner, even when they need you.

Whether or not codependency emerges in your relationship, you will have certain uncrossable lines and need to set fixed boundaries with consequences for crossing them. The trick to not letting a situation get that far is to first recognize and talk about what you want and don't want from your partner, while explaining how this connects to your needs.

It might be difficult for your partner to hear that they are pushing your limits, and it might be hard or impossible for them to give you what you want. They must understand, however, which of your needs are going unmet and how that feels; otherwise, they will have no reason to even try. Your unmet needs might relate to your partner's lack of engagement in treatment, lack of motivation, negativity, lying and broken promises, self-medication, poor self-care, overspending, irritability/anger, changes in libido, reckless behavior, and/or lack of social engagement.

The framework of Nonviolent Communication (NVC) helps enormously with this kind of communication, and I recommend reading Marshall B. Rosenberg's book *Nonviolent Communication: A Language of Life*. NVC makes a distinction between needs and requests. Needs are human and universal: the need for connection, the need for honesty, the need for independence, the need for a meaningful life, and so on. A request asks for a specific action or strategy that would meet a need (e.g., "Would you please come home by 10 p.m.?").

NVC recognizes that we can't always agree to others' requests. If you can help your partner understand how their behavior conflicts with your needs, though, you can think creatively together about a request that feels realistic and doable for them (e.g., "I need to feel considered. If you can't come home by 10 p.m., would you agree to let me know?").

In Real Life

Anthony and Simone just had their first effective conversation ever about Simone's resistance to taking medication. They both feel heard and seen. Anthony now understands that having to take meds feels like a violation of Simone's need for independence, and Simone understands that when she lies about taking them, it violates Anthony's need to be trusted. Simone agrees to Anthony's request to stop hiding what she's doing, and Anthony agrees not to tell Simone what to do. It's a good start.

Talk About It

Effectively talking about your unmet needs starts with an objective, neutral observation of the facts, such as: "We haven't had sex in two weeks, and we usually do it more often. I know you're trying a new medication and you mentioned you think it's lowered your sex drive."

Next, let your partner know how this makes you feel without making any statements about their intentions: "The fact that you're trying something new makes me feel hopeful, but I'm also feeling lonely and undesirable." Connect the fact and your feeling with a need: "I do need to feel hopeful, but I also need physical intimacy."

Then make a request: "Would you be willing to tell your doctor about the side effect and see if they can suggest an alternative?" When making a request, be prepared for your partner to say no. Maybe there's an alternative you could negotiate: "Would you be willing to cuddle, even if you don't feel like making love?"

Have a sense of how strongly you want to push back if your partner resists. If you want to stay firm, repeat your request. Ignore attacks or diversions in the conversation: "I hear you, and I know I also have things I'm not taking care of, but I'm focused on this right now. Would you be willing to call your doctor?"

If you can't negotiate a request they'll agree to, remind them of your need: "I understand you don't want to try another med and that cuddling is too hard for you sometimes. I'm at a loss. What can we do about my need for physical intimacy?" Don't agree to disagree: "Maybe we can't figure it out right now, but I know there's a limit here for me. If we don't do anything, it will drive me away from you, and I don't want that. I'd like to talk about this again." Follow up at a later time.

If Behaviors Spin Out of Control

Acknowledging and accepting that your partner's illness attacks their willpower and their judgment can help you see bipolar disorder as a common enemy. However, it shouldn't be an excuse for overlooking their behavior. Excuses and explanations are irrelevant and distracting when the impact of the behavior is unacceptable. The more extreme the behavior, the more crucial it becomes for you to insist that your partner not cross the line. At a certain point, you'll need to be prepared to leave if they can't stop (more on this in chapter 9).

Stopping out-of-control behaviors requires outlining clear consequences (ones your partner won't like) that are tied to the behaviors you find unacceptable. Effective use of consequences requires careful thought and planning. State the consequences your partner will face for unacceptable behaviors during a calm moment, when you have your partner's full attention. Most important—and this cannot be overstated—*you must follow through*. Empty threats actually increase unwanted behaviors because they send the message that you may not object as strongly as you say you do.

Don't underestimate how hard it will be to remain firm when it's time to enforce a consequence. It will require you to cause your partner emotional pain, which will be hard for you to bear. They may go to great lengths to talk you out of it, make you feel guilty, or even try to hurt you back.

It gets even harder when the consequence is a withdrawal of your support, closeness, or commitment to the relationship. Remember to be very specific, clear, and firm. Don't threaten to end the relationship based on a particular crossed boundary unless you are 100 percent committed to doing so and are certain you will stick to your commitment. If you decide to end your relationship (as we'll discuss in chapter 9), this should be a carefully considered decision based on an accumulation of factors, not simply the last straw.

You must be specific and clear when describing the unacceptable behavior and consequences. When your partner crosses the line, you must both be able to recognize it immediately and know exactly how you will respond. Here are some examples of vague versus clear and specific statements:

Vague statement: "I won't stand for any more of your temper tantrums."

Clear statement: "You can't hit or throw things here. Next time you do that, I will walk out of the house."

Vague statement: "Stop being mean to me or I won't spend time with you anymore."

Clear statement: "Calling me a 'stupid idiot' is unacceptable. Next time you do that, I won't talk to you for the rest of the day."

Always remember that everything with bipolar disorder operates on a continuum (page 19). If you know your partner can go to the extreme in some way, outline various boundaries and consequences to match your partner's behavior if it moves in that direction. The following are some common troubling behaviors you may see and some approaches on how to handle the situation and state the consequences.

Financial

The combination of impaired judgment and poor impulse control during an episode of mood elevation can lead to excessive spending, gambling, poor investments, taking on debt, and other financial difficulties or even disasters.

You can formulate smart, preventive measures by learning from past behavior: How will your partner most likely spend money if they become symptomatic?

If your partner has had significant problems with excessive spending that sneaks up on them (or you), you will need to create a system of checks and balances together. For instance, you can agree that discretionary spending has to be a joint decision anytime it exceeds a certain amount. During an acute episode, you may need to take your partner's credit cards and phone away. They will not be happy about this at the time, but they may thank you later. Either way, their financial situation will remain intact.

If you feel there is a real danger that your partner could cause financial ruin, it may make sense to keep your finances separate or at least restrict your partner's access to your savings. Having assets in a joint account means either one of you can take everything out at any time. A banker, financial advisor, or attorney can advise you on how to plan so you can shut down or limit your partner's access to bank accounts or credit if need be. Setting up these kinds of boundaries will probably be triggering for your partner because they might feel you don't trust them. If you think it's the wise thing to do, though, don't let them talk you out of it. When it comes to financial well-being, there is a lot at stake.

Sexuality and Infidelity

Loss of libido can accompany depression and can also be a side effect of some medications for bipolar disorder. On the other side, hypersexuality (increased or more frequent sexual desire) is a common symptom of mood elevation. The additional symptoms of poor impulse control and lack of good judgment can lead to behaviors that negatively impact trust and intimacy. Risk of sexually transmitted infections (STIs), pregnancy, and affairs that hurt both you and other people are additional risks your partner poses if they behave irresponsibly in this arena.

Here are some examples of ways to state your boundaries with regard to a few common scenarios in this category:

Loss of libido: "I know this happens when you're depressed, but your loss of sexual energy makes me feel unwanted, and my sexual needs are going unmet. I need us to keep talking about this creatively instead of ignoring it, so we can find ways to address my needs."

Demanding sex from you: "I felt pressured into having sex, and that's not okay with me. I need you to back off when I tell you that I'm not in the mood. If you do that again, we'll be sleeping separately for the next month."

Hiding use of pornography: "I'm not comfortable with your hiding parts of your sex life from me. Maybe I wouldn't be comfortable with what you're doing, I don't know, but you need to let me in so we can talk about it. If you feel like you can't talk to me or can't control your use, I need you to get some professional help."

Infidelity: Don't make any assumptions here. Make sure you and your partner have a clear and explicit understanding of what is and is not allowed. Be clear with yourself and your partner what the consequences will be if they break the rules. The consequences might be different if you discover they're having an emotional affair, a one-night stand, or an ongoing sexual affair, for instance. The truth may be that you don't know what you will do. You could say, "If you were to break these basic rules of intimacy and trust that our relationship depends on, I don't know what I'd do." If you are 100 percent certain that a particular behavior would end your relationship no matter what, you can state that consequence.

In Real Life

Cynthia got herpes from Richard even though they've been married for years. He clearly acquired it elsewhere and brought it home. He's denying it, but she's caught him cheating more than once. It always happens when he's hypomanic, and afterward, he's racked with guilt. Last time, she told him their marriage would be over if he was ever unfaithful again, and now he is begging her to stay. She actually believes this time he'll change, but she's believed that before. She promised herself she wouldn't go back on her word. Heartbroken, she begins to pack her bags.

Substance Abuse

If your partner is addicted to alcohol, cannabis, or other substances, this will make it difficult for them to manage their bipolar disorder and they need to be willing to work on it. Even if they're working hard on their recovery, though, relapses are common. Setting up clear boundaries and consequences will help, but even if they suffer terrible consequences, your partner may well repeat the behavior at some point. You will need to ask yourself whether or not you can live with this possibility (we'll get to this more in chapter 9). In the meantime, here are some examples of effective boundary-setting:

Using drugs/alcohol immoderately: "We need to agree on how to measure what is a reasonable amount for you to drink/use. If you find you can't stick to that, I need you to get some help with it."

Lying about use: "I can't police your behavior. I need to know you're getting help from someone you feel comfortable talking to without lying."

Drinking, using drugs, or being under the influence while in the home or around children: "You can't behave this way in our home. If you do, I will ask you to leave and not come back until you're sober and ready to stop using." You can also set a proactive time restriction: "I'm not willing to live with you if you're drinking more than once a week," or "You can visit the kids on Tuesdays and Thursdays, as long as you're sober."

Friends drinking/using drugs in the home: "They can't do that here, and they can't come over if they're already high or drunk. I will tell them to leave, and if they won't, I'll call the police. This is my house, too."

Asking you to lie or "cover" for them: "I won't do that. You're responsible for your own mess."

Asking for money: "I'll help you pay for treatment, but I won't give you any more money."

Ending up in jail: "I won't bail you out or pay for a lawyer. You're responsible for the consequences of your behavior."

Stealing from you: "Either you find somewhere else to stay or I'm moving out. If I can't trust you around my things, we can't live together."

Explosive and Aggressive Behavior

Irritability, poor impulse control, and lack of insight are common symptoms of mood episodes, and angry outbursts are not uncommon for some people with bipolar disorder. Even if it is a result of a mood episode, however, you do not have to tolerate your partner losing their temper, especially if they direct their anger at you or your children. The following are some examples of boundaries to establish when explosive and aggressive behavior has been present:

Increased irritability: "When you snap at me, I feel criticized, which leaves me feeling bad about myself and angry at you. Sometimes I feel you are more irritable than usual and not really aware of it. I'm not saying I'm always right, but I would like you to hear me out nondefensively and reflect on it if I tell you I'm experiencing you this way."

Lost temper, aggression: "When you lose your temper, I feel attacked and scared, and I'm not okay with this. I need you to create and follow through on a concrete plan to work on controlling your temper. Please think about this and tell me what you're going to do about it by the end of this week."

Physical aggression: If your partner is physically forceful or threatening with you or if you are frightened, get away from them immediately and/or call 911. Once you are physically safe, call and consult with the 24/7 National Domestic Violence line (the Hotline; 1-800-799-7233). Consider taking out a restraining order. If you choose to speak with your partner again, say, "You may never hit me or anyone else around me. If you do that again, I will call the police."

In Real Life

Naima is sick of apologizing to Dalil. He constantly complains that "you're stressing me out," and this becomes his excuse for everything, from binge drinking to punching holes in the wall. Naima often blames herself, but when things get really bad, she can see he is having an episode. She doesn't want to go on like this forever—things have to change. Once he sleeps it off this time, she is going to set a strong boundary: Either Dalil goes to rehab by this Friday, or she is going to move out.

The Relationship among Codependency, Abuse, and Controlling Behaviors

The dynamic of codependency is driven by fear of losing the other person. At its worst, it can become a desperate cycle for both partners. Low self-esteem, avoidance, denial, and excessive control and compliance patterns are frequent features of codependent relationships and play a central role in most abusive relationships as well. Domestic abuse is a pattern of coercive and controlling behaviors, which can include constant criticism, putdowns, name-calling, humiliation, blame-shifting, coercion, threats or intimidation, using economic or other means of power to exert control, or using jealousy to justify controlling actions. Abusive relationships do not necessarily involve physical violence.

Abusive behavior is *not* a symptom of bipolar disorder, but it may be exacerbated by the illness and should not go unmentioned in a chapter about boundaries. Intimate partner abuse is life-threatening and an unacceptable violation of basic human rights. There is a common misconception that verbal or emotional abuse is less serious or "not that big of a deal" compared to physical abuse. If your partner is emotionally abusive, however, your safety is at risk, because abusive behaviors tend to worsen over time, with physical violence often emerging unexpectedly.

If your partner is consistently abusive, the wisest course of action for you will most likely be to figure out how to leave safely and then do so. If they become abusive only during mood episodes, you still may need to leave. You cannot be responsible for the care of an abusive partner. If you think your partner may be abusive, you will need advice tailored to your situation, so don't hesitate any longer: Seek immediate consultation with a mental health or domestic violence ▶

professional. The easiest way to start is the Hotline, a free service that has an excellent educational website: TheHotline.org. Counselors are available 24/7 for nonemergency calls (1-800-799-7233), live chat, and text. There are also helpful materials to read, including those listed in the resource section of the website, that can help you better understand abusive behaviors.

Write It Down

This chapter discusses many upsetting behaviors and explores how to observe your limits, establishing boundaries and consequences as necessary. In your journal, list the behaviors you worry about and identify boundaries and consequences for each. Don't wait any longer to talk with your partner if you think any of these behaviors could realistically happen, whether or not they've happened in the past.

Take a Mindful Minute

While events do spiral out of control in some relationships (whether or not bipolar disorder is present), most, if not all, of the scenarios in this chapter will never happen to you. But perhaps some already have. Knowing how much you and your partner care about each other doesn't always make the situation better and can even make it feel worse; the uncertainty of whether or not you will need to follow through on consequences can feel scary. Give yourself credit for your courage in facing this head-on. Addressing this now will benefit both you and your partner, but that doesn't mean it's going to be easy. Your thoughtfulness about your relationship and your willingness to communicate with your partner put you ahead of the game.

For now, take a stress-relieving break from these thoughts. If possible, go for a walk somewhere beautiful like a park or maybe just around your neighborhood and find something in nature to focus on. If you can't get outside, simply spend some time with an indoor plant or flowers.

Take a few deep breaths and allow yourself to sink into nature by engaging all your senses. Notice the colors and scents, the touch of the leaves, the sounds around you, the breeze on your skin, etc. Be mindful of your thoughts, feelings, and physical sensations just as they are in this moment without judgment, and simply breathe.

Chapter 8

When Children Are Involved

If you and/or your partner have children, your partner's bipolar disorder will ultimately have an effect on them, just as it has on you. It's easy to imagine a variety of negative impacts, but that doesn't mean the negatives will outweigh the positives. As with any difficulty, children are largely affected by how adults in their life cope with it, so modeling helpful behavior may have more of a lasting impact on your children than anything else. In this chapter, we'll discuss how to help your children understand bipolar disorder and its impact on your family, as well as how you can help them cope with it.

No Secrets

Because of the stigma and misunderstandings around bipolar disorder, your partner will have to decide what works best for them in terms of disclosing their illness to others. When it comes to your family, though, it would be virtually impossible to keep it a secret forever. Instead, it would become "the elephant in the room," and the longer it goes unmentioned, the scarier it can be for a child. Denying your partner's diagnosis could actually be harmful to your children, because they will detect not only that something is wrong but also that grown-ups, for some reason, are denying or evading the truth.

Dramatically changing moods, long episodes of depression, unusual behaviors, and interpersonal conflict may confuse and frighten children, especially if your partner's irritability or ability to function fluctuates unpredictably. Kids may have intense feelings they don't understand in response. They may experience shock, "check out," or seek to numb themselves. They may even act out.

If a parent cannot take care of themselves or if they lean too heavily on their children to meet their needs, children may feel called to "parent" their parents. Unhealthy family dynamics, including the codependency between two adults (page 108) can have long-term effects on children, contributing to dysfunction in their own intimate relationships as they grow.

A family where bipolar disorder is present is far from unique in this way. Some version of these kinds of problems impact many if not most families. But by helping your children understand what's happening in their family now, you will create protective emotional safety for them and strengthen their own mental health and relationships now and into the future.

A caregiver who is upset or losing control activates a child's threat-detection system. Children know when something is wrong, and they pay close attention, working to stay safe, figure out what's happening, and predict what will happen next. Kids are tuned in to emotional dynamics ("What's really going on?") on the most basic level: They feel it in their body. They may not know why, but they can tell when grown-ups around them are upset, and they will feel upset as a result.

Like adults, kids are generally able to function normally after feeling upset. To process their feelings, however, they need a helpful framework in which to understand them. Otherwise, the feelings fester, becoming linked to unhelpful thoughts that give the child a negative self-concept or scare them unnecessarily. You can help your kids process their feelings by acknowledging the reality of what they know to be true: Yes, something doesn't feel good. Let them know that it's okay to talk about the problem, and it's also okay if they don't want to talk about it. You can help by answering their questions truthfully. You can also help them learn to name their feelings and to know that it is completely okay to feel the way they do.

Every parent has lost emotional control around their child and regretted it. It's hard for kids to understand they may not be the cause of our upset. We adults generally hold it together, but sometimes we can't, whether or not we have bipolar disorder. Daily stressors build up and up, and suddenly, we lose control and let it all out. When this happens, there is always some immediate, proximate cause, the proverbial last straw.

When something a child does becomes the last straw for a grown-up, the child logically concludes that they have caused the grown-up intense distress. If a caregiver's degree of upset is outsized or unpredictable, children feel anxious or confused. Helping them understand and put names to the emotional dynamics makes them feel safer and more in control. Usually it's enough just to say, "I'm sorry I yelled, sweetie. I'm not actually angry with you. I'm stressed about something at work that has nothing to do with you."

Stress is fairly easy for children to understand, but bipolar disorder is a lot more complicated. Helping them understand your partner's behavioral shifts will be a process that happens over time. This process should be closely coordinated with your partner. You should discuss together how and when to talk with your children about it and what you plan to say or have already discussed with your kids. Based on your child's age, certain information may be inappropriate or too much for them to take in, so what you decide to share should be tailored to what your children can both tolerate and understand.

In Real Life

Ashleigh returned home from work to find her husband, Josh, staring numbly at a video game on the TV. He seemed irritable when she asked, "Where are the kids?" A few moments later, she found the kids building racetracks in their bedroom, and they burst into tears. "Daddy is grumpy and ignoring us," the older one said. "We tried to bring him a snack and play a game with him—we even tried to wash the dishes—but he was mad. We couldn't do anything to cheer him up."

Talk About It

Explaining to children that a family member is coping with bipolar disorder will help them understand what is happening and increase their sense of safety.

Set aside some time to talk with your partner about how the two of you want to address bipolar disorder with your children. You can use the following questions as a guide:

- "How has the bipolar disorder affected our children so far?"

- "What do they know already?"

- "What do we want them to know?"

- "How would we like the kids to feel after the conversation?"

- "What about having this conversation with them scares us or makes us uncomfortable?"

- "Are there any parts of this conversation we want to role-play or practice beforehand?"

- "How does it feel to talk with each other about this challenge?"

What You Can Do to Help Your Child

We all want to create a safe and nurturing environment for our children. Bipolar disorder is only one of many factors in life that can make this goal challenging. There are some common strategies discussed in this section that can help create a safe environment for children in any family, along with some specific points about bipolar disorder.

Foster Open Communication

Creating an environment that encourages open communication is one of the best ways you can help your children. Growing up is filled with countless unknowns and many questions. Children need to know that they can share their inner life and ask whatever questions they have, not because they need them all answered but because they need the security of knowing there is a grown-up who will try to listen to them and meet their needs.

Fostering open communication means tuning in to what your children are feeling and trying to facilitate their general emotional understanding of family dynamics. Ask your kids if they have any questions about what's happening, and allow them to feel whatever they are feeling without trying to change it. Fostering open communication also means respecting their signals around whether or not they want to talk or would rather talk another time. If you want to initiate a conversation, do it somewhere that feels comfortable and private for the child: their bedroom, perhaps, or while driving together in the car.

Fostering open communication also means not pretending that everything is okay when your partner clearly isn't or when you are preoccupied with helping them manage the illness. Knowing that your partner "isn't feeling well" or "is sick right now" will help kids understand when your partner is behaving abnormally. Be honest with them, while sticking to an appropriate level of detail. If you're not sure how to answer a question, you can just say so: "That's an important question, and I'm not sure what the answer is. Let me think about it, and we'll talk again later."

Encourage Sharing Emotions

It's often difficult for kids to name their feelings, and they may feel uncomfortable sharing them. Be gentle and curious, validating their experience as normal and understandable. Reflect back to them what you heard them say until you've got it right: "It sounds like you feel [insert feeling/emotion here]. Did I get that right?" If they let you in on some difficult feelings, hold yourself back from trying to make them feel better right away. Once you're sure you understand what they're feeling, you can say, "I get it" or "Of course you feel that way, I understand," and then wait. More is likely to follow.

Naming your own feelings can help your children know it's okay for them also to open up and share their feelings with you. Here are some examples of how you can help start these conversations:

- "It makes me sad to see your mom so down. Do you feel that way, too?"

- "Your dad hasn't been feeling well, and that's been hard on all of us. Sometimes I just feel overwhelmed—like the other day when I started crying, remember? Do you feel overwhelmed sometimes?"

- "Did you notice when your dad snapped at me this morning about the eggs? I felt really angry at him. He's not usually like that, but I know he gets cranky with you, too, sometimes. How does it feel when that happens?"

- "We all try our best to help Mommy, and we have to balance that with everything else we need to take care of. Sometimes I feel guilty—like this morning, when I told her she had to get her own breakfast. Do you ever feel guilty when she's feeling sad?"

Develop Coping Skills

Modeling healthy coping skills for your children and helping them develop their own are essential tasks for a parent. Use your own coping skills with intention and awareness and explicitly describe them to your children as you use them. Here are a few examples to get you started:

- "I'm feeling a little overwhelmed. I'm going to take a short walk to clear my head and reset. I'll be back in 20 minutes."

- "I'm upset and I've got some problem-solving to do, but I need to calm down a bit first and change my mood. Want to watch some funny cat videos together?"

- "It's been a tough day. I'm going make myself some tea. Can I make you a hot chocolate?"

- "Sometimes I get discouraged when I feel like your dad will stay depressed forever. I have to remind myself that it may take a bit of time, but his doctors and his medicine should help him feel better soon."

You can help children develop coping skills by helping them notice moments when they're struggling. If you see (or believe) they are stressed out or overwhelmed, ask them, "Are you feeling overwhelmed?" Then make a suggestion for something they might choose to do: jumping jacks (or another form of exercise), a snack, a shower or bath, etc. In calmer moments, you can educate them more about coping skills by brainstorming with them a list of stress-relievers that might work best for them.

Take Your Child to See a Therapist

A therapist can help your child sort through their emotions, respond effectively to their environment, and develop coping skills. Your child may benefit greatly from a safe place to talk about what they're experiencing, especially if they are feeling worried, afraid, ashamed, sad, guilty, or any other difficult feelings due to what's happening at home.

As we've discussed, it's sometimes hard for children to express their questions and concerns, and your child's therapist may be able to help them do this. They may also be able to give you some information about handling living with a parent who has bipolar disorder. As mentioned, children whose biological parent has bipolar disorder are at increased risk of developing the condition; working with a therapist may reduce this risk by helping your child learn how to cope with stress and develop protective habits.

Create a Safe Environment

First and foremost, children must be safe. If your children are in physical danger or are subject to verbal or psychological abuse due to your partner's behavior, you must find a way to put a stop to this immediately. This may mean contacting social services, a therapist, a doctor, or other trained experts. If you don't know where to begin, start with your child's primary care doctor. If a crisis is currently happening, call 911. If you think it is possible that your partner could become abusive, this should be your first concern: Turn to page 119 to review the discussion on codependency, abuse, and controlling behaviors.

If your partner becomes acutely manic, psychotic, or otherwise out of control, it may be better for your children to stay with a trusted relative or close friend until the situation resolves. Seeing their parent in this kind of altered state can be scary and even traumatic. If your partner is in the hospital, consider the impact of bringing children to visit them. There may be pros and cons, but you can go by yourself first to get a sense of how to prepare the kids if you decide they should join you.

Make sure your partner takes extreme caution to ensure that their medication is completely inaccessible to children. Kids are notorious for dangerously mistaking medication for candy, and this risk could be exacerbated if they watch your partner take medication regularly. Taken in quantity, many of these drugs can be deadly, and you and your partner should explain this clearly to your children. Your partner can reduce the risk by using a pillbox that contains a week's supply and keeping it somewhere the children cannot access it; the rest of their medication can be kept in a safe or a locked cabinet.

In Real Life

Nico is a sensitive boy. He prefers to avoid sad books and movies and expresses a lot of concern when "Mommy is sad." Dana and her partner, Luke, decide that explaining the condition will help Nico handle harder times. "It will help him relax knowing that nothing's wrong with our family or our day," they agree. Now Luke can tell Nico, "You know everyone has an inner grouch. The bipolar disorder is making Mommy extra grouchy lately. She is practicing some ways to calm that inner grouch."

Answering Your Child's Questions

Let's now address some of the common questions your children may ask. Regardless of the question, it's helpful to continually emphasize that your partner "*has* bipolar disorder" rather than "*is* bipolar." This seems like a subtle distinction, but saying, "The bipolar disorder makes Daddy irritable" carries a different meaning than "Daddy is irritable." By talking about what the bipolar disorder does, instead of what your partner does, you help everyone remember that your partner is separate from their diagnosis and that the whole family has the power to unite against the illness.

How to talk to kids about bipolar disorder depends upon their age. Preschool-age children need little detail; they need simple, concrete information that focuses on things they can directly see. Older children will have more questions, which tend to be plain and simple. They want to know the "why" behind what they see and hear. They may also have worries based on incorrect assumptions. They need simple, direct, and honest answers to their questions. They also need reassurance that they will be taken care of no matter what and that your partner is getting the help they need. Teenagers can engage in conversations about bipolar disorder on a more sophisticated, almost adult, level and may have more specific and challenging questions. They will want you to express interest in their opinion, and if you don't know the answer to something, they will respect you for admitting it.

In the following sections, you will find some categories of questions you may face and ideas for how you might respond. Ultimately, use your judgment to make your way through these conversations. Don't be hard on yourself if you feel like you've said the wrong thing, too much, or too little. It's not about making the conversation perfect; it's about *having* the conversation. If you feel you've said the wrong thing, you can always correct yourself later on.

"Why is Mom/Dad so sad?"

Your child might want to know why your partner is feeling intense emotions. Here are a few examples of what you can say to help them understand:

- "Your mom/dad isn't feeling well right now."

- "They feel sick in their feelings (or 'are having an episode'). A doctor is helping them. They will get better."

"Does Mom/Dad still love me?"

Your child might be concerned that their mom or dad doesn't want or love them during mood episodes. Here is an example of what to say:

- "Mom/Dad absolutely loves you. When they're not feeling well, though, they may have a hard time showing it."

"What is bipolar disorder?"

Your child will be curious to know what bipolar disorder is and what's involved. Here are a few ways to help them better understand:

- "Bipolar disorder is 'a chemical imbalance in the brain.' You can call it a 'brain illness' or a 'sickness in the brain.'"

- "Bipolar disorder affects how people feel and think and how they behave."

- "Bipolar disorder creates up-and-down moods at different times. Mom/Dad may feel just fine most of the time, but if they're not feeling well, their mood and energy change."

- "These moods come in episodes/phases/periods of time that can last a while—days, weeks, or months."

- "When Dad/Mom feels depressed or down, the bipolar disorder takes away their energy and slows them down; when they are feeling up, it speeds them up with lots of energy."

- "You can tell if Mom/Dad is depressed because the bipolar disorder makes them feel [sad/flat/cranky] and you will see them [fill in the blank]. You can tell when it makes them feel up, because the bipolar disorder makes them feel [great/excited/cranky] and you can see [fill in the blank]."

- "When the bipolar disorder makes your mom/dad feel extra good or up, they like the way that feels, but sometimes it gets out of control. We have a plan for what to do if that happens."

"Can bipolar disorder be cured? Is it contagious? Will I get it?"

Your child may not understand the concept of a chronic condition or illness. Here are some ways to explain it:

- "Bipolar disorder is a condition that a person has all their life. But having bipolar disorder doesn't mean they are sick all the time; it just means they *can* get sick in a certain way."

- "A person with bipolar disorder can get sick more than once during their life, but then they get better. It doesn't stop their body from working, the way a heart attack or cancer might."

- "There are treatments that help with bipolar disorder, including medicine and therapy. With treatment, most people can stay well most of the time. If they get sick again, they can be treated again."

- "Mom/Dad is getting treatment from a doctor, and they will get better. We don't know how long that will take, and they might get sick again in the future, but they will always get better."

- "Most people with bipolar disorder live a normal life and no one would ever know they have this condition."

- "Bipolar disorder is not contagious; it's not something you can catch."

- "Doctors aren't sure why some people develop bipolar disorder. It's more likely if it runs in the family, but there's a much greater chance that family members *won't* develop it. Plenty of people are the first in their family to get it."

"Do other people know about Mom/Dad's bipolar disorder?"

It can be hard living with someone who has bipolar disorder, especially when they are unstable, and your child may wonder who they can talk to about it. Explain to them the limits you and your partner hold around discussing their bipolar disorder with others. To help them understand, here are a few ways to answer this question:

- "Lots of people have bipolar disorder, and it's nothing to be ashamed of, but this is a private matter. It's important for us to talk about how it makes us feel with one another (and with the child's therapist, if they have one)."

- "Bipolar disorder is different for everyone, and many people don't understand that. They often make assumptions based on what they see in movies or on TV. We have decided not to tell anyone other than [name the people who know]."

- "When Dad/Mom is feeling sick, they might say or do things that make kids or other grown-ups feel bad. They might act in ways that are embarrassing. It's important to remember that this might be happening because they're not feeling well, but you don't need to make excuses for their behavior. You can talk to us (or your therapist or other trusted adult who knows) about it."

"What should I do?"

Your child may want to help in some way, but it's not their job to take care of their parents. Here are a few ways to respond to this question:

- "When you know and understand more, that actually helps everyone, because we might accidentally assume you understand something that you don't. We want to know if you're confused or aren't getting what you need. If there's something you wonder about, and you ask us about it, that's actually helpful."

- "It's not your responsibility to help Dad/Mom feel better. Your job is just to be a kid, and my job is to take care of you. Taking care of Dad/Mom when they're not feeling well is their doctor's job."

- "Let me or another grown-up know if you're having trouble or need help. Therapists can help everyone. If you want to talk to one yourself, we can make that happen."

- "It's not your job to worry or watch out, but I know you might worry anyway and worries feel better when there's a plan. You can tell Dad/Mom might be feeling sick if [fill in the blank]. If you're worried about them, you come to me. Here are names and numbers of other adults you can call [write these down], and here's what to do in an emergency [write this down]."

In Real Life

After Chloe's kids found medication in the bathroom, she and her new partner, Brady, decided she would tell them about his bipolar disorder. Chloe took them out for ice cream and explained that although they know Brady as healthy and happy, he wasn't always that way. She told them about his past depressions and explained that he is committed to staying well, which means taking medication every day. Chloe and Brady arranged a time for him to acknowledge to the kids that he knows they know and to give them a chance to ask questions.

Write It Down

If you've had a talk about bipolar disorder with your kids, you may want to check in with them again to see how much they understand or give them more information. Let them know you are all going to have a conversation about bipolar disorder and you're going to do it by playing a little game. Have your child (with your help, if they want) make a list of any thoughts, feelings, or questions they have for your partner, and ask your partner to make a list of anything they want your kids to know. Then, as a family, compare the lists to see if there is overlap, and talk about those items first. Then, talk about the rest.

Considering Having Children?

Your partner's children will have a roughly 10 percent chance of developing bipolar disorder (in contrast to 1 to 2 percent in the general population). You may be wondering if that means you should not have children together or should foster or adopt a child instead. There are no simple answers to this question, because there are real and complex reasons that people ask it, and having a child means taking responsibility for their life.

In addition to increased risk of your child developing bipolar disorder, hormonal changes and other stressors involved in pregnancy can trigger mood episodes, as can the stress and sleep deprivation of caring for an infant. There is increased risk of postpartum depression (which can occur in men as well as women). Furthermore, if your partner is a woman, there are implications for her medication and she should consult her psychiatrist if considering pregnancy: She may need to stop or change her medication during pregnancy and breastfeeding, which could dramatically increase her risk of an episode.

Despite the risks, many couples with bipolar disorder choose to have children for the same reasons other couples do. After all, there are countless risks involved in having a child, and parents pass down genetically increased risk for a variety of illnesses—bipolar disorder is far from unique in this regard. If a parent with bipolar disorder has a child who develops bipolar disorder, the family may be better able to help them with all the knowledge they have gained about how to manage it successfully.

The following questions may help you think about whether and how your partner's bipolar disorder might ▶

impact your decision to have children. You may want to talk these questions over with your partner as well.

- Can you predict what would happen if your partner has an episode? How likely is this to happen? (You may want to discuss this question together with their psychiatrist.)

- Is your partner committed to successfully managing their illness?

- How many episodes have they had?

- How long has it been since the last one?

- Have you seen an episode firsthand?

- Do you have a plan for what you'll do if it happens?

- If your partner has a mood episode, is there a backup support system? (For instance, are there people and financial resources available to help?)

Take a Mindful Minute

We put so much pressure on ourselves to be good parents, protect our kids, and help them grow. I hope the material in this chapter is helpful, but I know it strikes at some of the most fearful places in any parent's heart. The best thing you can do for your children is make sure you are in a position to help them by taking care of your own needs. Your kids depend on you to stay grounded and centered, and this means you need to focus on self-care. One of the best forms of self-care is taking time for mindfulness exercises, such as meditation. Here is one that will help you center yourself. You'll need a candle and a dark room.

1. Set a timer for 5 or 10 minutes and light the candle.

2. From a comfortable distance away, let your eyes sink into the flame.

3. Observe the hues of light as they pulse and dance. Take in the contours of the flame, as well as what's going on within the flame.

4. Notice the wick glow and watch the wax as it melts. As you focus on the flame, take note of what's happening in your peripheral vision, too.

5. Let go of thoughts as they arise by returning your full attention to the flame. Do this until the timer goes off.

This exercise can transport you to a magical, serene place. Meditation and other mindfulness exercises are excellent forms of self-care because they can help you learn how to turn your attention away from worrisome thoughts and find calm. Making time for mindful moments every day is one lesson I hope you take from this book.

Chapter 9

How Is Your Relationship?

So, you made it to the last chapter, and you have every right to be proud of yourself! Now that you've taken time to digest the information and work through the exercises, you have a more informed foundation from which to ask yourself how your relationship is doing, in light of your partner's bipolar disorder. This is probably the underlying question that brought you here in the first place. In this chapter, we'll dive into assessing your relationship by evaluating the good, the bad, and how you are managing the condition together. I'll make some suggestions for improving your relationship, such as how to talk issues over with your partner and perhaps consider couples counseling. I'll also discuss the hard decision you may face over whether to end the relationship.

Taking Stock

Overanalyzing your relationship can get in the way of enjoying the positive moments you and your partner can and do share. You need to resolve conflicts and hurts as they arise, but your relationship's health depends on being present for the good moments. That said, it's important not to blindly accept the current state of your relationship or assume unquestioningly that you want to continue it. Being partnered isn't a reality carved in stone; it's something that's happening over time, moment by moment. Particularly if you're going through a difficult period, you may find yourself needing to make the decision to stay again and again.

So, you need to know how to step back and take stock of how things are going. It's natural to think about how bad your relationship is when things are difficult, but taking stock of your relationship isn't something to wait on until you're deciding whether or not to end it. This is something you should do during moments of calm, when you can look at the relationship as a whole. Only then can you appreciate the parts of it that make you happy and identify pieces you wish were different.

The following questions are drawn from a scientifically validated assessment of intimate partner relationship functioning called the Timberlawn Couple and Family Evaluation Scales–Self-Report (TCFES-SR). Very few couples score high in all areas, as all relationships have room for growth; in fact, relationships grow and become stronger when couples learn from challenges and mistakes. These questions are suitable for any relationship:

- "How do we share power and is it comfortable? Do we compete? Negotiate? Compromise? Is one of us 'in charge'?"

- "Do we share similar interests, beliefs, activities, friends, values, and pleasurable time?"

- "Is it easy for us to understand or listen to each other's values, opinions, and ideas?"

- "Are we able to deal with problems or find solutions to difficult situations?"

- "How do we express and respond to each other's emotions? Do either of us frequently feel rejected or invalidated?"

- "Are my and my partner's tone and mood with each other mostly negative or positive?"

- "How often do our talks result in problems or conflict?"

- "Do disagreements or conflicts between us usually get resolved?"

- "Is my partner able to be honest with me and vice versa?"

The following questions are specific to your partner's bipolar disorder:

- "How does my partner talk with me about bipolar disorder?"

- "Has my partner truly accepted their diagnosis?"

- "Are we able to communicate about what is needed to manage the bipolar disorder effectively? Do we share a vision for that?"

- "Have we been able to talk about my role in managing the illness and how I can be supportive?"

- "Is my partner engaged in treatment and working effectively with their doctor?"

- "Does my partner struggle with taking their medication as prescribed?"

- "Is my partner honest with me, their doctors, and themselves about their mood, medication, and substance use?"

- "Does my partner struggle with substance abuse as well as bipolar disorder?"

- "Has my partner's condition ever threatened my or my family's health and safety? Is it negatively affecting my children or others I love?"

As you answered all of these questions, did you focus mostly on shortcomings or strengths? Reflect on why you might have done that, then reread the questions while focusing on the opposite for more insight.

In addition to thinking about your answers, reflecting on your relationship with a trusted friend or family member can help you sort out your thoughts. Choose someone who agrees to listen in a neutral way and will let you process your feelings without injecting their own, even if this goes against their instincts. If you don't have anyone in your life like this and you're troubled about your relationship, it may be worth speaking with a therapist.

Checking In with Your Partner

Many couples share feelings about their relationship most frequently during high-conflict moments when it isn't always constructive. Rather than waiting for everything to spill out when tempers are hot, you can intentionally set aside time to take stock of your relationship with your partner in a calmer moment. Don't try to launch into a check-in out of the blue. You'll want to have taken time to think before doing this, and your partner will want to do the same. Start with telling them you want to check in, then ask when would work for them.

I encourage couples to have regularly scheduled check-ins, weekly or monthly. This way, it doesn't feel like you're asking for a check-in because your partner did something "wrong." To start a regular schedule, always plan your next meeting before you wrap up the one you're having.

When asking for a check-in, reassure your partner that your intention is not to end the relationship but rather to strengthen it by giving it some attention. (Even if ending the relationship isn't on your mind, your partner might worry that it is.) Tell them you want to make space to appreciate them, not just identify things that aren't working well.

Start the conversation by expressing at least one thing about your partner that you're deeply grateful for but don't tell them often enough. As you move into the room-for-growth part, continue to give positive feedback. You can use the "sandwich method," surrounding the "meat" of constructive criticism with the "bread" of appreciations and positive sentiments. Another framework for this is "roses, thorns, and buds," where each of you first calls out some nice things about the relationship (roses), then speaks to pain points (thorns), and ends by identifying something you are looking forward to doing or sharing together going forward (buds).

When you talk about the "thorns," try to present them in the context of your own unmet needs rather than complaints about your partner's behavior (page 111). Instead of communicating that your partner is doing something wrong, explore how the two of you are discussing each other's needs and why a particular behavior is distressing you. This strategy will decrease defensiveness in your partner and will also allow you to take responsibility for your own part in the dynamic.

Couples Therapy

If you and your partner decide to do some intensive work together on your relationship, a couples therapist may help. Seeing a couples therapist is different from seeing your own therapist or one of you attending the other one's individual therapy. A couples therapist's job is not to treat either of your individual mental health needs but rather to treat the health of your relationship. A couples therapist can help you and your partner communicate, work through conflicts, and shift the balance of positive versus negative interactions. A couples therapist can also act as a neutral party to help you have productive conversations about conflicts.

Whether your relationship is in trouble or just needs a tune-up, couples therapy can potentially improve it. If your interactions are becoming frequently intolerable or you are thinking seriously about giving up on your relationship, this is a clear sign that something must be done. If you are still willing to work on it, you might suggest couples therapy. If your partner resists, you can tell them they will need to choose couples therapy or end the relationship if that's the consequence you decide is right for you.

Couples therapy is unlikely to be productive if your partner is experiencing an acute episode of mood elevation, especially if you are just beginning with a new couples therapist. It's the top priority for your partner to engage in treatment for bipolar disorder at this time. If you cannot get them to seek treatment, you can go to a couples therapist with the aim of getting them into treatment, but in my experience this doesn't often work. Couples therapy is best when your partner's mood is more stable but can still help if they are depressed.

In Real Life

After four difficult years with Vivienne, Cristiana decided she'd had it. She didn't want to break up right before the vacation they're taking for Vivienne's birthday, though, and now she doesn't know what to do. Ten days together with no conflicts . . . She can't believe how well they're getting along. Vivienne volunteered that she's decided to take treatment seriously for the first time ever. Cristiana needs to think. She'll talk it through with her cousin Veronica when she gets home. Veronica never judges or tells her what to do. Somehow, she just gets it.

Write It Down ～～～～～～～～～

Label four pages in your journal: "Past Week," "Past Year," "Past Five Years," and "Next Five Years." Think over each of these periods of time and spend some time writing in each. Ask yourself: What has your partner brought to your life (in the past week, the past year, the past five years)? How might your life have been different if your partner weren't in it (the past week, the past year, the past five years)? Make sure to notice both the richness and the challenges they have brought to your life. How do you envision the next five years? What are your hopes and fears? How do you want your relationship to grow?

When the Relationship Is Thriving

This book largely addresses how to meet the challenges that bipolar disorder presents for your relationship, but you would hardly read it if things were all bad. You're here, I imagine, because your relationship has been full of good times, too. You've walked together, you've laughed together, and you've been there for each other. You've shared secrets, pleasures, and sorrows. You've talked about the world, your life, your family, your beliefs and values, and the people you see every day. You've made plans for the future together. You've had each other's backs. Perhaps at times you've reached a state of flow together when a whole day passes without even noticing the time. You know each other better than almost anyone else in the world. You may have even brought children into the world together.

The fact that your partner has bipolar disorder doesn't make your relationship "disordered." On the contrary, as we've discussed, if you work together and your partner works diligently on managing their illness, the challenge can bring you closer. This may already be happening.

If taking stock of your relationship returns a resounding or even partial, "Hey, we're doing pretty darn well," then take a moment—or a bunch of moments—to celebrate. Tell your friends, tell your family, tell your partner: Appreciate the relationship out loud! Noticing that things are going well opens space to note the positive ways you've met your challenges and to reflect on what made the difference. Not every couple would have coped as well.

Make note of the circumstances that surround the good times, so you can re-create them intentionally when things get hard. When your partner is feeling well, what does your compatibility look like? Is it:

- More music and laughter around the house?

- Exercising and going on hiking or other outdoor adventures together?

- Watching TV, playing a game, or reading together?

- Spending less time on your phones and other screens?

- Having more physically intimate evenings?

- Planning for weekend "dates" or an overnight getaway?

- Wanting to be more social together with others, or having more just-the-two-of-you time?

Note as well how your partner positively manages their bipolar disorder:

- What are the strengths that see them through?

- Do they show resilience and the ability to recommit to wellness?

- Do they have friends and family who show up in supportive ways when needed?

- How have your partner and their support system supported you and your needs that arise as a result of the bipolar disorder?

Pay special attention to naming the plans, coping styles, and ways you rely on each other that have helped you manage the condition:

- What do you do as a team that keeps things stable?

- How do you respond together when your partner becomes symptomatic?

- How do you reach out when you need each other?

- How do you nourish the relationship in an ongoing way?

Knowing the answers to these questions will help you return to your strengths if they are challenged in the future.

The initial exhilaration that comes with falling in love doesn't last forever. The falling-for-each-other part is easy; building a satisfying, long-lasting relationship is harder. Couples come up against the many challenges of life, and even the most loving people hurt each other sometimes. You and your partner will have to rediscover your connection again and again.

An illness like bipolar disorder brings the potential to wear away at a relationship, with or without the presence of acute episodes. Even if things are pretty rosy, the condition may have created some rocky times for your relationship, and there may be more difficulties ahead. So, make sure to pause and notice when things are good.

Do your best to be fully present with your partner when they are well, making time to enjoy each other's company. Soak in the richness of your relationship and remember why you are together in the first place. This will mean something different to each couple, but whatever it means to the two of you, jump on the chance to do it: Go on a date, do hobbies together, spend time with your children, play with your pets, pick out flowers to grow in the garden, etc. Capitalize on the good times when they're here.

In Real Life

With Nia emotionally stable for nearly three years, Damien thought the worst was behind them, but she's recently started using drugs, skipping her meds, and lying about it again. When he confronts her, she breaks down in tears and recommits to their agreements, but Damien senses another period of instability and stress on the horizon. He can't believe he's thinking of leaving her when she's so sick, but he also doesn't know if he can take another round of this. "No more second chances" is what he said, but he's torn. They've been through too many good times for him to walk away this instant. Once she stabilizes, he'll insist on couples therapy and on Nia reevaluating her medication with her psychiatrist.

If It's Time to End the Relationship

Even after trying the exercises in this book and asking your partner for help, things may not be getting better. You may have considered couples therapy, but either your partner isn't willing to try it or you've tried and it didn't help. Reflecting on the questions raised in this chapter may lead you to a somber question: Is it time for you to leave the relationship?

If your partner's behavior is abusive or threatens the physical or mental health of anyone in your home, including you and your children, it is time to leave the relationship now, at least until that changes. But even if that's not the case, deciding to end the relationship may still be the right thing to do. If you believe the bipolar disorder is making your relationship intolerable, ask yourself these questions:

- Does your partner understand that the bipolar disorder is negatively impacting your children and/or causing the relationship to be intolerable for you? Do they understand why? Are they willing to listen and try to understand? Are they willing to do anything about it?

- Is your partner able to stay consistently engaged in treatment? Are they willing to commit to staying engaged? Do you believe they can? Do you think they actually believe this will be better for them and for your relationship, or are they just doing it at your insistence?

- Do their health-care providers think they have the ability to get better at doing what they need to do to manage the illness over time? How likely is it, according to the opinion of their health-care providers, that the course of your partner's illness (frequency and severity of episodes) could improve over time?

- Is there room for improvement in how you're working together to manage the illness? Is your partner willing to do their part?

- Does your partner consistently put their own self-destructive habits before your or your children's needs and well-being? Are they committed to looking out for your needs, even with their bipolar disorder?

- If they are making commitments to you, do you think they have the strength to follow through on those commitments and not give up when things get harder?

You cannot control your partner's future choices or the course of their illness. If you want to stay, ask yourself:

- What if your partner tries their hardest, but nonetheless loses control and their behavior become unmanageable? What if things get worse?

- Are you willing to take on the unpredictability and risk this implies for your future or your children's future?

- Do you feel that your partner's life is more important than yours? Do you have any lines that can't be crossed? Are you letting things slide that in the past you would have called deal-breakers?

- Are you willing and able to look out for yourself, to walk away from the relationship in the future if you need to do so for your own sake?

- If you have children, how is your partner's bipolar disorder impacting them?

Though your partner has an illness and needs help, it's a mistake to operate as though there are no limits to what you are willing to do. Your life and your mental health matter, and you alone are responsible for ensuring your own well-being.

If you have children, you are also responsible for their well-being. Your happiness, your quality of life, and the things you value could be suffering a degree of deprivation you no longer wish to bear. Your sense of integrity or self-esteem may be too degraded, and the resilience of your love for your partner may be damaged beyond repair. You may simply be tired of hanging in there and feel it is no longer worth it. Leaving your partner may be the right choice. It may be the best of two bad choices, but the decision is ultimately up to you.

Leaving a partner with a serious illness is one of the most heart-wrenching decisions imaginable. It comes with many conflicting and intense emotions. Even if your partner is causing you great distress or even harm, you may still love them deeply. Or you may feel bewildered, sad, or guilty that you no longer love them, or at least not as much as you once did. Part of you may want to hurt them; part of you may feel that you cannot bear hurting them. You may worry they cannot live without you (and they may have threatened as much). You may be afraid to lose your partner, fearing your own loneliness. You may feel shame at the idea that you have "failed." You may have children and want to stay with your partner for their sake.

The guilt in particular can feel unbearable, especially if your partner has developed a dependency on you. If caring for those who need help is a deeply held value of yours, you will feel even guiltier. While this feeling is valid and understandable, that doesn't mean it's reasonable. A healthy relationship is interdependent, not codependent, which means you are allowed to have your needs met, too.

If you truly believe it's your responsibility to sacrifice everything and anything to ease your partner's pain, then you and I can agree to disagree, but don't tell yourself you're staying for your partner. Make the sacrifice with your eyes open and take ownership of the decision. Otherwise, your choice will lead to more resentment and more guilt.

Your partner's bipolar disorder is not their fault. This is true, tragic, and real. They may follow every single treatment recommendation and still become unstable. When the illness strikes and an episode happens, it may cause them to behave in ways they never otherwise would and to make choices they regret. Unfair as it may be, they remain accountable for these choices, and the choices may have tragic consequences. Loss of your relationship and loss of your care may be, and sometimes must be, one of those tragedies.

In Real Life

Alison has stood by Nate through eight rocky years since his diagnosis, supporting him through every depression and a two-week hospitalization. Committed to their relationship and his well-being, she has been part of his therapy and medication journey. During a recent manic episode, though, Nate slept with another woman. Alison had warned him that she would not forgive this behavior. She knows he "didn't mean to do it," and it's hard to leave when he's still recovering, but he has a therapist to look after him. She's allowed to have her limits, and he's not her responsibility. She is leaving.

Talk About It

If you've decided to end your relationship after careful consideration, take some time to prepare for the conversation. Writing and rehearsing a script ahead of time can be helpful if there are things you want to make sure to convey. When the time comes, you'll be less nervous and prepared to be gentle and respectful of your partner's need to express themselves, too.

Your partner may accept your decision, expressing sadness, hurt, anger, or even relief. They may also, however, try to talk you out of it. When they realize you are actually ending the relationship, they may be more motivated to change their behavior than ever before. You may believe their promise to change, and it may be hard to resist their pleas. Remember that, in taking stock of your relationship, you've considered your partner's ability to change and decided that, no matter how hard they are willing to try, the relationship is not healthy for you anymore.

Don't put it off because you're waiting for the right time. If you know the struggle to maintain the relationship is over, you owe it to your partner to let them know as soon as possible. Here are a few things you may want to say:

- "I need to talk to you about something . . . This is really hard because I care about you so much and I want to be here to support you."

- "I hate the bipolar disorder. We've tried to work on it together, but it has been so destructive to our relationship."

- "I know you don't have the luxury to walk away from bipolar disorder, and I feel so awful leaving you with it, but it's destroying my sanity, and I can't let it do that."

Take a Mindful Minute

The journey through this book cannot have been easy, but you have stayed the course. Take a moment to recognize your accomplishment. I hope this book will help you improve your relationship and your life, but the work laid out here can't be done all at once. As you look over all the suggestions, such as talking to your partner or keeping a journal, you might think about breaking down some of the tips into more manageable pieces. For example, when you ask your partner to work with you on answering some questions, you might start with only two or three questions rather than tackling them all at once.

In this chapter, I asked you to take stock of your relationship and your broader situation, an assessment that may have raised hope for the future but perhaps also raised some doubts. This is hard work and can be stressful, especially when you think about your needs going unmet or uncertainty about the future. Remember that focusing too much or too long on analyzing your relationship isn't healthy. It's probably best to take a break from focusing on it, at least for the day, and do something to de-stress.

One of the most important lessons I hope you take from this book is that self-empowerment and self-care are the keys to supporting your partner. When it comes to self-care, exercise is one of the best, across-the-board recommendations we health-care providers know. It has proven benefits for physical health, mood, and clarity of mind. If you have a form of exercise that works for you, now is a great time to enjoy it! If, like many of us, you have struggled to incorporate exercise as a long-lasting habit, start small.

If you haven't taken a walk, let alone a jog, in the past seven days, deciding to run three miles a day starting tomorrow, will set you up to fail. Instead, set a more realistic initial goal—how about two short walks outdoors this coming week? If you meet that goal, it will give you a boost of confidence. Your next goal can be to maintain it for another week. Raise the bar slowly, maybe adding one long walk to your two short walks and so on. Always keep your goals realistic and achievable.

There is no better place to start than taking a few deep breaths as you open the front door for a walk outside. Practice deep breathing on your walk and perhaps focus on one of your senses for the first part of your walk, switching to another sense before you head home. Listen to the birds, look up at the sky, take a few moments to smell the flowers, and relax knowing you've completed a book that has given you many new tools to move forward in your relationship. First things first, though—you simply need to get started. How about that first walk sometime today or this evening?

Resources

Organizations with Support Groups

DailyStrength Bipolar Disorder Support Group

DailyStrength.org/group/bipolar-disorder

A social network centered on support groups.

Depression and Bipolar Support Alliance (DBSA)

DBSAlliance.org

Offers regularly scheduled, peer-led family and friends support groups (both in-person and online). More information is available at DBSAlliance.org/support/chapters-and-support-groups.

National Alliance on Mental Illness (NAMI)

NAMI.org

Organizes peer-led family support groups. More information is available at NAMI.org/support-education/support-groups/nami-family-support-group. For more on the free, innovative family-to-family program (a structured, research-supported, eight-session program conducted by NAMI-trained family members), visit NAMI.org/support-education/mental-health-education/nami-family-to-family.

7 Cups Bipolar, Schizophrenia, and Psychosis Support

7Cups.com/home/bipolar

Provides online therapy and free support to people experiencing emotional distress by connecting them with trained listeners.

Finding a Therapist

Psychology Today

PsychologyToday.com

An extensive directory of therapists, with excellent search filters to target what you're looking for. Most therapists these days have a listing here.

Open Path Psychotherapy Collective

OpenPathCollective.org

A directory of therapists who offer low-fee or sliding-scale pricing.

Advekit

Advekit.com

Simplifies the process by suggesting only three possible therapists. The service can help you submit insurance claims, including for out-of-network providers. Available in several states, but not nationwide.

Theravive

Theravive.com

Another therapist directory service.

Therapy Tribe

TherapyTribe.com

Therapist directory service and wellness tools.

Network Therapy

NetworkTherapy.com

Another therapist directory service with resources and articles.

Websites

Mood Surfing

MoodSurfing.com

Devoted to creative, non-pathologizing ways to conceptual-
ize bipolar and other mood disorders.

moodgym

moodgym.com.au

Self-help CBT resources.

NAMI—Bipolar Disorder

NAMI.org/about-mental-illness/mental-health-conditions
/bipolar-disorder

Good, basic information about bipolar disorder—a quick read
for anyone who wants a brief education.

Psych Education

PsychEducation.org

Information about mental health, with a focus on mood
disorders.

Bipolar Network News

BipolarNews.org

Provides updates on bipolar disorder research and treatment.

DBT Self-Help

DBTSelfHelp.com

Explains DBT skills that can be used to regulate emotions.

The Centre for Addiction and Mental Health (CAMH)—When a Parent Has Bipolar Disorder

CAMH.ca/en/health-info/guides-and-publications/when -a-parent-has-bipolar-disorder

A guide for parents with bipolar disorder to talk with their children about the condition.

Books

The Bipolar Bear Family: When a Parent Has Bipolar Disorder by Angela Holloway (AuthorHouse, 2006)

Bipolar Disorder: A Guide for Patients and Families, 4th Edition, by Francis Mark Mondimore, MD (Johns Hopkins University Press, 2020)

The Dialectical Behavior Therapy Skills Workbook for Bipolar Disorder: Using DBT to Regain Control of Your Emotions and Your Life by Sheri Van Dijk, MSW (New Harbinger Publications, 2009)

The Rainbow Angels: A Story for Children about Bipolar Disorder by Madeleine Kelly (Two Trees Media, 2001)

An Unquiet Mind: A Memoir of Moods and Madness by Kay Redfield Jamison (Vintage Books, 1995)

Wellness Recovery Action Plan (WRAP), 5th Edition, by Mary Ellen Copeland (Peach Press, 2011)

When Someone You Love Has a Mental Illness: A Handbook for Family, Friends, and Caregivers, New Revised and Expanded by Rebecca Woolis, MFT (Jeremy Tarcher/ Putnam, 1992)

References

Agarkar, Smita, Nahla Mahgoub, and Robert C. Young. "Use of Transcranial Magnetic Stimulation in Bipolar Disorder." *Journal of Neuropsychiatry and Clinical Neurosciences* 23, no. 2 (Spring 2011): E12–13. doi:10.1176/appi.neuropsych .23.2.E12.

American Psychiatric Association. *Diagnostic and Statistical Manual of Mental Disorders*. 5th ed. Philadelphia, PA: American Psychiatric Association, 2013.

Bahji, A., E. R. Hawken, A. A. Sepehry, C. A. Cabrera, and G. Vazquez. "ECT Beyond Unipolar Major Depression: Systematic Review and Meta-Analysis of Electroconvulsive Therapy in Bipolar Depression." *Acta Psychiatrica Scandinavica* 139, no. 3 (March 2019): 214–226. doi: 10.1111 /acps.12994.

Baldessarini, Ross J., Leonardo Tondo, and Gustavo H. Vázquez. "Pharmacological Treatment of Adult Bipolar Disorder." *Journal of Molecular Psychiatry* 24, no. 2 (February 2019): 198–217. doi: 10.1038/s41380-018-0044-2.

Basco, M. R., and A. J. Rush. *Cognitive-Behavioral Therapy for Bipolar Disorder*. 2nd ed. New York: The Guilford Press, 2007.

Bauer, Mark S., Linda McBride, William O. Williford, Henry Glick, Bruce Kinosian, Lori Altshuler, Thomas Beresford, Amy M. Kilbourne, and Martha Sajatovic. "Collaborative Care for Bipolar Disorder: Part I. Intervention and Implementation in a Randomized Effectiveness Trial." *Psychiatric Service* 57, no. 7 (July 2006): 927–936. doi: 10.1176/ ps.2006.57.7.927.

Bauer, Mark S., Linda McBride, William O. Williford, Henry Glick, Bruce Kinosian, Lori Altshuler, Thomas Beresford, Amy M. Kilbourne, and Martha Sajatovic. "Collaborative Care for Bipolar Disorder: Part II. Impact on Clinical Outcome, Function, and Costs." *Psychiatric Services* 57, no. 7 (July 2006): 937–945. doi: 10.1176/ps.2006.57.7.937.

Berk, Michael, Philippe Conus, Nellie Lucas, Karen Hallam, Gin S. Malhi, Seetal Dodd, Lakshmi N. Yatham, Alison Yung, and Pat McGorry. "Setting the Stage: From Prodrome to Treatment Resistance in Bipolar Disorder." *Bipolar Disorders* 9, no. 7 (November 2007): 671–678. doi: 10.1111/j.1399-5618.2007.00484.x.

Bonanno, George A. *The Other Side of Sadness: What the New Science of Bereavement Tells Us About Life After Loss.* New York: Basic Books, 2010.

Calhoun, Gina, and Dina McFalls. "WRAP for Everyday Lives." In *The Wellness Recovery Action Plan (WRAP)* by Mary Ellen Copeland. Sudbury, MA: Human Potential Press, 2018.

Castle, David, Carolynne White, James Chamberlain, Michael Berk, Lesley Berk, Sue Lauder, Greg Murray, Isaac Schweitzer, Leon Piterman, and Monica Gilbert. "Group-Based Psychosocial Intervention for Bipolar Disorder: Randomised Controlled Trial." *British Journal of Psychiatry* 196, no. 5 (May 2010): 383–388. doi: 10.1192/bjp.bp.108.058263.

Colom, Francesc, and Eduard Vieta. "A Perspective on the Use of Psychoeducation, Cognitive-Behavioral Therapy and Interpersonal Therapy For Bipolar Patients." *Bipolar Disorders* 6, no. 6 (December 2004): 480–486. doi: 10.1111/j.1399-5618.2004.00136.x.

Copeland, Mary Ellen. *The Wellness Recovery Action Plan (WRAP).* Revised Edition. Sudbury, MA: Human Potential Press, 2018.

Cotrena, Charles, Laura Damiani Branco, Flávio Milman Shansis, and Rochele Paz Fonseca. "Predictors of Quality of Life in Bipolar Disorder: A Path Analytical Study." *Psychiatry Research* 285 (February 2020): 112846.

Crowe, Marie, Kate Eggleston, Katie Douglas, and Richard J. Porter. "Effects of Psychotherapy on Comorbid Bipolar Disorder and Substance Use Disorder: A Systematic Review." *Bipolar Disorders* (July 2020).

Crowe, Marie, Maree Inder, Holly A. Swartz, Greg Murray, and Richard Porter. "Social Rhythm Therapy—A Potentially Translatable Psychosocial Intervention for Bipolar Disorder." *Bipolar Disorders* 22, no. 2 (March 2020): 121–127. doi: 10.1111/bdi.12840.

Culver, Jenifer L., and Laura C. Pratchett. "Adjunctive Psychosocial Interventions in the Management of Bipolar Disorders." In *Handbook of Diagnosis and Treatment of Bipolar Disorders*, edited by Terence A. Ketter, 661–676. Arlington, VA: American Psychiatric Publishing, Inc., 2010.

Dagani, Jessica, Ross Baldessarini, Giulia Signorini, Olav Nielssen, Giovanni de Girolamo, and Matthew Large. "The Age of Onset of Bipolar Disorders" In *The Age of Onset of Bipolar Disorders: Etiopathogenetic and Treatment Implications*, edited by Giovanni de Girolamo, Patrick D. McGorry, and Norman Sartorius, 75–110. Cham, Switzerland: Springer International, 2019.

De Barros Pellegrinelli, K., L. F. de O. Costa, K. I. D. Silval, V. V. Dias, M. C. Roso, M. Bandeira, F. Colom, and R. A. Moreno. "Efficacy of Psychoeducation on Symptomatic and Functional Recovery in Bipolar Disorder." *Acta Psychiatrica Scandinavica* 127, no. 2 (February 2013): 153–158. doi: 10.1111/acps.12007.

De Gregorio, Danilo, Justine P. Enns, Nicolas A. Nuñez, Luca Posa, and Gabriella Gobbi. "D-Lysergic Acid Diethylamide,

Psilocybin, and Other Classic Hallucinogens: Mechanism of Action and Potential Therapeutic Applications in Mood Disorders." *Progress in Brain Research* 242 (2018): 69–96. doi.org/10.1016/bs.pbr.2018.07.008.

Dome, Peter, Zoltan Rihmer, and Xenia Gonda. "Suicide Risk in Bipolar Disorder: A Brief Review." *Medicina* 55, no. 8 (August 2019): 403. doi: 10.3390/medicina55080403.

Duffy, Anne, Sarah Goodday, Charles Keown-Stoneman, and Paul Grof. "The Emergent Course of Bipolar Disorder: Observations over Two Decades from the Canadian High-Risk Offspring Cohort." *American Journal of Psychiatry* 176, no. 9 (September 2019): 720–729. doi: 10.1176/appi.ajp.2018.18040461.

Fast, Julie A., and John D. Preston, PsyD. *Loving Someone with Bipolar Disorder: Understanding & Helping Your Partner.* Oakland, CA: New Harbinger Publications, 2012.

Forman, Miloš, dir. *One Flew Over the Cuckoo's Nest*. Hollywood, CA: United Artists, 1975.

Fountoulakis, Konstantinos N., Lakshmi Yatham, Heinz Grunze, Eduard Vieta, Allan Young, Pierre Blier, Siegfried Kasper, and Hans Jurgen Moeller. "The International College of Neuro-Psychopharmacology (CINP) Treatment Guidelines for Bipolar Disorder in Adults (CINP-BD-2017), Part 2: Review, Grading of the Evidence, and a Precise Algorithm." *The International Journal of Neuropsychopharmacology* 20, no. 2 (February 2017): 121–179. doi.org/10.1093/ijnp/pyw100.

Fountoulakis, Konstantinos N., and Melina Siamouli. "Re: How Well Do Psychosocial Interventions Work in Bipolar Disorder?" *Canadian Journal of Psychiatry* 54, no. 8 (August 2009): 578. doi.org/10.1177/070674370905400813.

Frank, Ellen. *Treating Bipolar Disorder: A Clinician's Guide To Interpersonal And Social Rhythm Therapy*. New York: The Guilford Press, 2005.

Frank, Ellen, David J. Kupfer, and Michael E. Thase, et al. "Two-Year Outcomes for Interpersonal and Social Rhythm Therapy in Individuals with Bipolar I Disorder." *Archives of General Psychiatry* 62, no. 9 (September 2005): 996–1004. doi: 10.1001/archpsyc.62.9.996.

Gendlin, Eugene T. *Focusing*. Revised ed. New York: Bantam Books, 1981.

Gitlin, Michael. "Lithium Side Effects and Toxicity: Prevalence and Management Strategies." *International Journal of Bipolar Disorders* 4 (December 2016): 27. doi: 10.1186 /s40345-016-0068-y.

González, Isasi A, Enrique. Echeburúa, José María Limiñana, and Ana González-Pinto. "Psychoeducation and Cognitive -Behavioral Therapy for Patients with Refractory Bipolar Disorder: A 5-Year Controlled Clinical Trial." *European Psychiatry* 29, no. 3 (March 2014): 134–141. doi: 10.1016 /j.eurpsy.2012.11.002.

Goodwin, G. M., P. M. Haddad, I. N. Ferrier, J. K. Aronson, T. R. H. Barnes, A. Cipriani, D. R. Coghill, et al. "Evidence-Based Guidelines for Treating Bipolar Disorder: Revised Third Edition Recommendations from the British Association for Psychopharmacology." *Journal of Psychopharmacology* 30, no. 6 (June 2016): 495–553. doi .org/10.1177/0269881116636545.

Gordovez, Francis James A., and Francis J. McMahon. "The Genetics of Bipolar Disorder." *Molecular Psychiatry* 25, no. 3 (March 2020): 544–559. doi: 10.1038/s41380-019-0634-7.

Gottlieb, John F., Francesco Benedetti, Pierre A. Geoffroy, Tone E. G. Henriksen, Raymond W. Lam, Greg Murray, James Phelps, et al. "The Chronotherapeutic Treatment of Bipolar Disorders: A Systematic Review and Practice Recommendations from the ISBD Task Force on

Chronotherapy and Chronobiology." *Bipolar Disorders* 21, no. 8 (December 2019): 741–773. doi: 10.1111/bdi.12847.

Ionescu, Dawn F., David A. Luckenbaugh, Mark J. Niciu, Erica M. Richards, and Carlos A. Zarate. "A Single Infusion of Ketamine Improves Depression Scores in Patients with Anxious Bipolar Depression." *Bipolar Disorders* 17, no. 4 (June 2015): 438–443. doi: 10.1111/bdi.12277.

Jamison, Kay Redfield. *Touched with Fire: Manic-Depressive Illness and the Artistic Temperament*. New York: Simon & Schuster, 1993.

Jamison, Kay Redfield. *An Unquiet Mind: A Memoir of Moods and Madness.* New York: Simon & Schuster, 1995.

Kapczinski, Flávio, Vasco Videira Dias, Marcia Kauer-Sant'Anna, Benicio Noronha Frey, Rodrigo Grassi-Oliveira, Francesc Colom, and Michael Berk. "Clinical Implications of a Staging Model for Bipolar Disorders." *Expert Review of Neurotherapeutics* 9, no. 7 (July 2009): 957–66. doi: 10.1586/ern.09.31.

Kesey, Ken. *One Flew Over the Cuckoo's Nest.* New York: Viking Press, 1962.

Kübler-Ross, MD, Elisabeth. *On Death and Dying.* New York: Macmillan, 1969.

Lake, James, MD. *Alternative Treatments of Bipolar Disorder: Safe, Effective and Affordable Approaches and How to Use Them.* Independently published, 2019.

Lam, Dominic H., Steven H. Jones, and Peter Hayward. *Cognitive Therapy For Bipolar Disorder: A Therapist's Guide To Concepts, Methods And Practice*. West Sussex, UK: John Wiley & Sons, 2010.

Linehan, Marsha M.. *DBT Skills Training Handouts and Worksheets*. 2nd ed. New York: The Guilford Press, 2014.

López-Muñoz, Francisco, Winston W. Shen, Pilar D'Ocon, Alejandro Romero, and Álamo, Cecilio. "A History of the Pharmacological Treatment of Bipolar Disorder." *International Journal of Molecular Sciences* 19, no. 7 (July 2018): 2143. doi: 10.3390/ijms19072143.

Luft, Barrat. "Extrapyramidal Side Effects—Forgotten But Not Gone." *Graylands Hospital Drug Bulletin* 21, no.1 (March 2014): 1251–1323. ww2.health.wa.gov.au/-/media /Files/Corporate/general-documents/WATAG/WAPDC /Extrapyrimidal-side-effects-March-2014.pdf.

Mason, Brittany L., E. Sherwood Brown, and Paul E. Croarkin. "Historical Underpinnings of Bipolar Disorder Diagnostic Criteria." *Behavioral Sciences* 6, no. 3 (July 2016): 14. doi: 10.3390/bs6030014.

McIntyre, Roger S., and Joseph R. Calabrese. "Bipolar Depression: The Clinical Characteristics and Unmet Needs of a Complex Disorder." *Current Medical Research and Opinion* 35, no. 11 (November 2019): 1993-2005. doi: 10.1080/03007995.2019.1636017.

Meyer, T. D., and M. Hautzinger. "Cognitive Behaviour Therapy and Supportive Therapy for Bipolar Disorders: Relapse Rates for Treatment Period and 2-Year Follow-Up." *Psychological Medicine* 42, no. 7 (July 2012): 1429–1439. doi: 10.1017/S0033291711002522.

Miklowitz, David J. "Adjunctive Psychotherapy for Bipolar Disorder: State of the Evidence." *American Journal of Psychiatry* 165, no. 11 (November 2008): 1408–1419. doi: 10.1176/appi.ajp.2008.08040488.

Miklowitz, David J., and Bowen Chung. "Family-Focused Therapy for Bipolar Disorder: Reflections on 30 Years of Research." *Family Process* 55, no. 3 (September 2016): 483–499. doi: 10.1111/famp.12237.

Miklowitz, David J., Orestis Efthimiou, Toshi A. Furukawa, Jan Scott, Ross McLaren, John R. Geddes, and Andrea Cipriani. "Adjunctive Psychotherapy for Bipolar Disorder: A Systematic Review and Component Network Meta-analysis." *JAMA Psychiatry* (October 2020): e202993. doi: 10.1001/jamapsychiatry.2020.2993.

Miklowitz, David J., and Jan Scott. "Psychosocial Treatments for Bipolar Disorder: Cost-Effectiveness, Mediating Mechanisms, and Future Directions." *Bipolar Disorders* 11, suppl. 2 (June 2009): 110. doi: 10.1111/j.1399-5618.2009.00715.x.

Miller, Jacob N., and Donald W. Black. "Bipolar Disorder and Suicide: A Review." *Current Psychiatry Reports* 22, no. 2 (January 2020): 6. doi: 10.1007/s11920-020-1130-0.

Mondimor, Francis Mark. *Bipolar Disorder: A Guide for You and Your Loved Ones*. 4th ed. Baltimore, MA: Johns Hopkins Press, 2020.

Morris, Chad D., David J. Miklowitz, and Jeanette A. Waxmonsky. "Family-Focused Treatment for Bipolar Disorder in Adults and Youth." *Journal of Clinical Psychology* 63, no. 55 (May 2007): 433–445. doi: 10.1002/jclp.20359.

Myczkowski, Martin L., Adriano Silva, Marina Moreno, Leandro Valiengo, Beny Lafer, Ricardo A. Moreno, Frank Padberg, Wagner Gattaz, and Andre R. Brunoni. "Cognitive Outcomes of TMS Treatment in Bipolar Depression: Safety Data from a Randomized Controlled Trial." *Journal of Affective Disorders* 235 (August 2018): 20–26. doi: 10.1016/j.jad.2018.04.022.

Novick, Danielle M., and Holly A. Swartz. "Evidence-Based Psychotherapies for Bipolar Disorder." *Focus: The Journal of the American Psychiatric Association* 17, no. 3 (2019): 238–248.

Parikh, Sagar V., Ari Zaretsky, Serge Beaulieu, Lakshmi N. Yatham, L. Trevor Young, Irene Patelis-Siotis, Glenda M.

MacQueen, et al. "A Randomized Controlled Trial of Psychoeducation or Cognitive-Behavioral Therapy in Bipolar Disorder: A Canadian Network For Mood And Anxiety Treatments (CANMAT) Study." *Journal of Clinical Psychiatry* 73, no. 6 (June 2012): 803–810. doi: 10.4088/JCP.11m07343.

Perlis, Roy H., Michael J. Ostacher, Jayendra K. Patel, Lauren B. Marangell, Hongwei Zhang, Stephen R. Wisniewski, and Terence A. Ketter, et al. "Predictors of Recurrence in Bipolar Disorder: Primary Outcomes from the Systematic Treatment Enhancement Program for Bipolar Disorder (STEP-BD)." *American Journal of Psychiatry* 163, no. 2 (February 2006): 217–224. doi: 10.1176/appi.ajp.163.2.217.

Popovic, Dina, Maria Reinares, Jan Scott, Alessandra Nivoli, Andrea Murru, Isabella Pacchiarotti, Eduard Vieta, and Francesc Colom. "Polarity Index of Psychological Interventions in Maintenance Treatment of Bipolar Disorder." *Psychotherapy and Psychosomatics* 82, no. 5 (August 2013): 292–298. doi: 10.1159/000348447.

Post, Robert M. "The New News about Lithium: An Underutilized Treatment in the United States." *Neuropsychopharmacology* 43, no. 5 (April 2018): 1174–1179. doi.org/10.1038/npp.2017.238.

Post, Robert M., Lakshmi N. Yatham, Eduard Vieta, Michael Berk, and Andrew A. Nierenberg. "Beyond Evidence-Based Treatment of Bipolar Disorder: Rational Pragmatic Approaches to Management." *Bipolar Disorders* 21, no. 7 (November 2019): 650–659. doi: 10.1111/bdi.12813.

Rachid, Fady. "Maintenance Repetitive Transcranial Magnetic Stimulation (rTMS) for Relapse prevention in Patients with Depression: A Review." *Psychiatry Research* 262 (April 2018): 363–372. doi: 10.1016/j.psychres.2017.09.009.

Ramachandran, Vilayanur S., and Edward M. Hubbard. "Hearing Colors, Tasting Shapes." *Scientific American*. Published September 1, 2006. ScientificAmerican.com /article/hearing-colors-tasting-shapes.

Rea, Margaret M., Martha C. Tompson, David J. Miklowitz, Michael J. Goldstein, Sun Hwang, and Jim Mintz. "Family-Focused Treatment Versus Individual Treatment for Bipolar Disorder: Results of a Randomized Clinical Trial." *Journal of Consulting and Clinical Psychology* 71, no. 3 (June 2003): 482–492. doi: 10.1037/0022-006x.71.3.482.

Reinares, María, Anabel Martínez-Arán, and Eduard Vieta, eds. *Psychotherapy for Bipolar Disorders: An Integrative Approach*. Cambridge University Press, 2019.

Reinares, María, José Sánchez-Moreno, and Konstantinos N. Fountoulakis. "Psychosocial Interventions in Bipolar Disorder: What, For Whom, and When." *Journal of Affective Disorders* 156 (March 2014): 46–55. doi: 10.1016/j.jad .2013.12.017.

Rhee, Taeho Greg, Mark Olfson, Andrew A. Nierenberg, and Samuel T. Wilkinson. "20-Year Trends in the Pharmacologic Treatment of Bipolar Disorder by Psychiatrists in Outpatient Care Settings." *American Journal of Psychiatry* 177, no. 8 (August 2020): 706–715. doi: 10.1176/appi.ajp.2020 .19091000.

Romeo, Bruno, Walid Choucha, Philippe Fossati, and Jean-Yves Rotge. "Meta-Analysis of Short- and Mid-Term Efficacy of Ketamine in Unipolar and Bipolar Depression." *Psychiatry Research* 230, no. 2 (December 2015): 682–688. doi: 10.1016/j.psychres.2015.10.032.

Rong, Carola, Caroline Park, Joshua D. Rosenblat, Mehala Subramaniapillai, Hannah Zuckerman, Dominika Fus, and Yena L. Lee, et al. "Predictors of Response to Ketamine in Treatment Resistant Major Depressive Disorder and Bipolar Disorder." *International Journal of Environmental Research and Public Health* 15, no. 4 (April 2018): 771. doi.org/10.3390/ijerph15040771.

Rosenberg, Marshall B. *Nonviolent Communication: A Language of Life*. 3rd ed. Encinitas, CA: PuddleDancer Press, 2015.

Sadock, MD, Benjamin J., Virginia A. Sadock, MD, and Pedro Ruiz, MD. *Kaplan and Sadock's Synopsis of Psychiatry: Behavioral Sciences/Clinical Psychiatry*. 11th ed. Philadelphia, PA: Wolfers Kluwer, 2015.

Sajatovic, Martha, Marilyn Davies, and Debra R. Hrouda. "Enhancement of Treatment Adherence among Patients with Bipolar Disorder." *Psychiatric Services* 55, no. 3 (March 2004): 264–269. doi: 10.1176/appi.ps.55.3.264.

Scott, Jan, Francesc Colom, and Eduard Vieta. "A Meta-Analysis of Relapse Rates with Adjunctive Psychological Therapies Compared to Usual Psychiatric Treatment for Bipolar Disorders." *The International Journal of Neuropsychopharmacology* 10, no. 1 (February 2007): 123–129. doi: 10.1017/S1461145706006900.

Sureshkumar, Kailash, Srikala Bhrath, Kesavan Mralidharan, Preeti Sinha, and Shilpa Veluthethodi Sivaraman. "Role of High-Frequency Repetitive Transcranial Magnetic Stimulation in Augmentation of Treatment of Bipolar Depression." *Journal of ECT* 30, no. 4 (December 2014): 44–45. doi: 10.1097/YCT.0000000000000146.

Takeshima, Masahiro, Tomohiro Utsumi, Yumi Aoki, Zhe Wang, Masahiro Suzuki, Isa Okajima, Norio Watanabe, Koichiro Watanabe, and Yoshikazu Takaesu. "Efficacy and Safety of Bright Light Therapy for Manic and Depressive Symptoms in Patients with Bipolar Disorder: A Systematic Review and

Meta-Analysis." *Psychiatry and Clinical Neurosciences* 74, no. 4 (January 2020): 247–256. doi: 10.1111/pcn.12976.

Tavares, Diego, Martin Myczkowski, Rodrigo Alberto, Leandro Valiengo, Rosa Rios, Pedro Gordon, Bernardo Pereira Junior, et al. "Treatment of Bipolar Depression with Deep TMS (dTMS): Results from a Double-Blind, Randomized, Parallel Group, Sham-Controlled Clinical Trial." *Neuropsychopharmacology* 42, no. 13 (December 2017): 2593–2601. doi: 10.1038/npp.2017.26.

Tseng, Ping-Tao, Yen-Wen Chen, Kun-Yu Tu, Weilun Chung, Hung-Yu Wang, Ching-Kuan Wu, and Pao-Yen Lin. "Light Therapy in the Treatment of Patients with Bipolar Depression: A Meta-Analytic Study." *European Neuropsychopharmacology* 26, no. 6 (June 2016): 1037–1047. doi: 10.1016/j.euroneuro.2016.03.001.

Wang, Shengjun, Zhigang Zhang, Li Yao, Nannan Ding, Lingjie Jiang, and Yuchen Wu. "Bright Light Therapy in the Treatment of Patients with Bipolar Disorder: A Systematic Review and Meta-Analysis." *PLOS One* 15, no. 5 (May 2020): e0232798. doi: 10.1371/journal.pone.0232798.

Weinera, Richard D., and Irving M. Reti. "Key Updates in the Clinical Applications of Electroconvulsive Therapy." *International Review of Psychiatry* 29, no. 2 (April 2017): 54–62. doi: 10.1080/09540261.2017.1309362.

Won, Eunsoo, and Yong-Ku Kim. "An Oldie but Goodie: Lithium in the Treatment of Bipolar Disorder through Neuroprotective and Neurotrophic Mechanisms." *International Journal of Molecular Sciences* 18, no. 12 (December 2017): 2679. doi: 10.3390/ijms18122679.

Woolis, MFT, Rebecca. *When Someone You Love Has a Mental Illness: A Handbook for Friends, Family, and Caregivers.* 2nd ed. New York: Penguin, 2003.

Yatham, Lakshmi N., Sidney H. Kennedy, Sagar V. Parikh, Ayal Schaffer, David J. Bond, Benico N. Frey, and Verinder Sharma, et al. "Canadian Network for Mood and Anxiety Treatments and International Society for Bipolar Disorders 2018 Guidelines for the Management of Patients with Bipolar Disorder." *Bipolar Disorders* 20, no. 2 (March 2018): 97–170. doi: 10.1111/bdi.12609.

Young, L. Trevor. "What Exactly Is a Mood Stabilizer?" *Journal of Psychiatry and Neuroscience* 29, no. 2 (March 2004): 87–88. NCBI.NLM.NIH.gov/pmc/articles/PMC383340.

Index

Acknowledgments

A book like this can only be written on the basis of clinical experience, and I would know next to nothing on this topic without the many people who have come to my office seeking help. A therapist does their best to provide good treatment, but the gift is that brought by the patient: They give their therapist their trust. When a human being shares their heart and bares their soul, it is truly awe-inspiring, and I have had the privilege to receive this gift many times. I am grateful to all my patients for everything they have taught and continue to teach me. If I can share a bit of knowledge here to help others, it comes ultimately from them.

Whatever we learn is based on what we perceive, and what we perceive is molded by the lenses through which we see the world. As Dr. Thomas Lynch reminds us, "We see the world not as it is, but as we are." I will be forever grateful to my most influential supervisors, who molded my clinical lenses: Dr. Jessica Apfel, Dr. Timothy Brown, Dr. Don Capone, Dr. Rosemary Ellmer, Dr. F. Myron Hayes, Dr. Robert Holaway, Dr. Eugenie Hsu, Dr. Yvonne Klatt, and Dr. Sandra Macias.

I wrote this book while swimming in the most stimulating, nourishing clinical waters I can imagine. Working with my small group of colleagues at the Wise Mind Institute has been the most important professional development of my life. I learn from them daily in a practice united in methodology and purpose. I am grateful to everyone at Wise Mind and owe particular thanks to Dr. Alison Alderdice and Dr. Wes Pederson for extending the invitation to join. I am also grateful to Dr. Marsha Linehan and Dr. Thomas Lynch, who have shaped our institute and my clinical thinking, perhaps more than anyone else.

My foundation of research and expert knowledge began at the PGSP-Stanford PsyD Consortium in Palo Alto, California. I owe my greatest thanks to my dissertation advisors there, Dr. Jenifer Culver and Dr. Shelley Howell. They guided, pushed, and questioned me as I digested the primary literature on bipolar disorder, personality, temperament, and creativity. Dr. Terence Ketter welcomed me to the Bipolar Disorders Clinic at Stanford, making space for me to follow my interests and sharing not only his expertise and research but also his curiosity.

I owe a special thanks to Dr. Jeffrey Friedman, whose wisdom and expertise provided a critical pathway as well as a continual source of inspiration and guidance.

This book would not exist without my managing editor at Callisto Media, Samantha Holland. Her supportive guidance, steady hand, and incisive suggestions made this book a proud reality for me.

I am enormously grateful to my mother, Ruth Osterweis Selig, particularly for her help during the final stages of the project. She not only taught me to write during my younger years but also showed me the value of generosity and the importance of health, above all.

Saving the most important for last, I must thank my family. My children have been patient, understanding, and an ever-present source of love and joy. Their fortitude and resilience throughout our current pandemic has amazed and inspired me. My wife, Sarah, had no idea what she was in for when she agreed to support me through this project. She has shouldered the weight that followed with generosity and forgiveness, even during this difficult year, and for that I will always be grateful.

About the Author

 **William O. Selig, PsyD, MFA,** is a clinical psychologist practicing in the San Francisco Bay Area. He earned his doctorate from the PGSP-Stanford PsyD Consortium, writing his dissertation on bipolar disorder and creativity at Stanford University's Bipolar Disorders Clinic. He co-led a 2014 revision of the psychotherapy for bipolar disorder treatment track at Kaiser Permanente Psychiatry & Behavioral Health in Oakland, California, where he later cofounded the dialectical behavior therapy (DBT) program. Before becoming a psychologist, Dr. Selig worked for more than a decade as a stage director, producer, and actor in New York, Boston, and the Bay Area. He holds an MFA in stage directing from the Moscow Art Theater School/Harvard University and a BA from Harvard College.

Printed in the USA
CPSIA information can be obtained
at www.ICGtesting.com
BVHW012004070823
668326BV00003B/24